THE APPEARANCES OF OUR LORD
AFTER THE PASSION

THE

APPEARANCES OF OUR LORD AFTER THE PASSION

A STUDY IN
THE EARLIEST CHRISTIAN TRADITION

BY

HENRY BARCLAY SWETE, D.D.

REGIUS PROFESSOR OF DIVINITY IN THE UNIVERSITY OF CAMBRIDGE

παρέστησεν ἑαυτὸν ζῶντα μετὰ τὸ παθεῖν αὐτόν

WIPF & STOCK · Eugene, Oregon

Wipf and Stock Publishers
199 W 8th Ave, Suite 3
Eugene, OR 97401

The Appearances of Our Lord After the Passion
A Study in the Earliest Christian Tradition
By Swete, Henry Barclay
ISBN 13: 978-1-5326-1748-5
Publication date 1/30/2017
Previously published by Macmillan, 1908

TO

E. L. S.

THE THIRD DAY
HE ROSE AGAIN ACCORDING TO THE SCRIPTURES
AND ASCENDED INTO HEAVEN,
AND SITTETH ON THE RIGHT HAND OF
THE FATHER.

FOREWORD

THESE pages were written during the last summer vacation in the hope that a simple narrative of the Appearances of the risen Lord, based on a study of the documents, might be welcome to readers of the English New Testament, and especially to those who undertake the responsible work of imparting Biblical knowledge in schools or to classes of adults. The text of the work has been rigidly closed against the admission of Greek words, although references to the original are given in the footnotes for the sake of the daily growing number of readers and teachers of the English Bible who possess some acquaintance with Greek.

Few things are more important than that Christian people should learn to realize the fact of our Lord's risen and ascended life, and its relation to their own lives and hopes. It is happy for us that year by year the recurrence of Eastertide offers an opportunity for kindling a fresh interest in this great subject. The writer will be glad indeed if this little book should help any to enter more fully into the spirit of that Queen of Seasons.

CAMBRIDGE,

Advent, 1907.

CONTENTS

PAGE

INTRODUCTION,   -   -   -   -   -   -   -   xi

APPEARANCES DURING THE FORTY DAYS :

    I.   TO THE WOMEN AT THE TOMB, -   -   -   1

   II.   TO SIMON PETER,   -   -   -   -   -   13

  III.   TO CLEOPAS AND ANOTHER,   -   -   -   17

  IV.   TO THE TEN AND OTHERS, -   -   -   -   26

   V.   TO THOMAS AND THE REST,   -   -   -   41

  VI.   TO THE SEVEN, BY THE LAKE, -   -   -   51

  VII.   TO THE ELEVEN, ON THE HILLS,   -   -   67

VIII.   TO JAMES,   -   -   -   -   -   -   -   86

  IX.   TO THE ELEVEN, BEFORE ASCENDING,   -   91

APPEARANCES AFTER THE ASCENSION :

    I.   TO STEPHEN,   -   -   -   -   -   -   113

   II.   TO SAUL,   -   -   -   -   -   -   -   120

  III.   TO JOHN,   -   -   -   -   -   -   -   132

POSTSCRIPT,   -   -   -   -   -   .   -   -   141

INDEX, -   -   -   -   -   -   -   -   -   -   150

INTRODUCTION

1. For our knowledge of the facts connected with the life of Christ we depend upon the recollections of the Apostles and other immediate followers of the Lord. These reminiscences were delivered to their first converts during the days that followed the Pentecost, in the ordinary intercourse of life, or in instructions given by word of mouth to catechumens or to Christian congregations. *They delivered them unto us*, S. Luke bears witness,[1] *which from the beginning were eyewitnesses and ministers of the word.* The tradition thus created was reduced to writing by not a few of those who received it.[2] As the Christian student to-day reads and ponders the surviving records, he makes it his aim to win back from them, so far as he can, the primitive impression of the works and words, the sufferings and the triumphs of Jesus Christ.

2. Not the least precious of these recollections are those which are now to be examined, and which relate to the appearances of the risen Lord after His Passion. The available evidence on this subject is to be found almost exclusively in the New Testament, where it may be collected from the Gospels, the Acts, the Epistles of S. Paul, and the Apocalypse. Of these documents the oldest is the first Epistle of S. Paul to the Corinthians,

---

[1] Lc. i. 2. [2] *Ibid.* 1.

which was written little more than five and twenty years after the Crucifixion.[1] Next comes the Gospel according to S. Mark; S. Matthew, S. Luke (Gospel and Acts), and S. John (Gospel and Apocalypse) follow at uncertain intervals, but all probably before the end of the first century. The precise date of the composition of these books, however, is not of the first importance; we are more concerned to know what opportunities the writers possessed of getting at the facts from the original witnesses or from those who had heard their story.

3. The evidence of S. Paul[2] leaves no reason for doubting that on five occasions, at least, witnesses who were still living when he wrote believed themselves to have seen the risen Lord during the six weeks that followed His death. With two of these witnesses, S. Peter and S. James, the Lord's brother, S. Paul had an interview at Jerusalem three years after his conversion, and it is reasonable to suppose that he then heard their experiences from their own lips.[3] But important as it is to the Christian apologist, S. Paul's statement is of little service to one who would construct a narrative of the appearances. His purpose is merely to summarize teaching which he had given at Corinth when he first preached the Gospel there. Accordingly, he enumerates only the most important of the appearances, or those of which he had first-hand information, and he does not enter into any particulars. His list will be useful to us only so far as it helps us to verify, and at one or two points supplement, the narratives of the Gospels.

4. It is to the Gospels, then, that we must turn for

[1] About A.D. 56.   [2] In 1 Cor. xv. 5-7.

[3] See Gal. i. 18 f., and Bp. Chase's remarks in *Cambridge Theological Essays*, p. 392.

details. As we have said, they are all later than S. Paul's first letter to Corinth; nor is it possible to speak with the same confidence as to the sources upon which they draw. But an early second century belief, which modern research tends to confirm, attributed the substance of S. Mark's Gospel to the teaching of S. Peter;[1] and if S. Mark had been preserved intact, we should undoubtedly have possessed in his last chapter a document of the highest value. Unhappily the original S. Mark comes to an abrupt end in the middle of the first post-Resurrection scene,[2] and the appendix, which begins at Mark xvi. 9, is by a later writer of secondary authority. It is probable, however, that S. Matthew has, according to his custom, worked up into his last chapter much of the matter contained in the lost ending of S. Mark, adding certain incidents for which he relied upon his own resources.[3] S. Luke begins on the same general lines as S. Mark and S. Matthew, but presently goes his own way,[4] and contributes one of the most convincing of the post-Resurrection narratives, for which he was probably indebted to first-hand testimony. Lastly, the fourth Gospel, which, here as elsewhere, is almost wholly independent of the synoptists, supplies accounts of four great manifestations of the risen Lord. These, however much they may have been idealized by the writer, bear every mark of being based on the personal knowledge of the great Christian teacher to whom we owe at least the substance of the book.[5]

[1] See the writer's *S. Mark*, p. xxiii f.

[2] With the words *for they were afraid* (xvi. 8).

[3] On the authorship of S. Matthew see W. C. Allen in the *Critical International Commentary*.

[4] Lc. xxiv. 13 ff.

[5] As to the appendix which forms *c*. xxi. see xxi. 24, and p. 54, note 2.

5. From this brief statement it will be clear that the Gospel records of the appearances, considered as evidence, are not all of equal value. The last twelve verses of S. Mark, for example, are the work of a writer whose name is not certainly known,[1] and whose information can scarcely be held to be as trustworthy as that of the interpreter of S. Peter. The Palestinian writer of the first Gospel has apparently relied here and there on rumours current at Jerusalem in his own time, which may or may not have had a place in the original tradition. It is at least probable that S. Luke adheres less closely to the original story in his earlier and later scenes[2] than in the graphic incident which fills the middle of his last chapter.[3] And the closing chapters of S. John's Gospel may, like much else in that wonderful book, have taken some of their colour from the author's own mind. It is fair to recognize such inequalities in the evidence, and to make due allowance for them.

6. As we cannot claim for the narratives of our Gospels an immunity from the subtle changes which oral tradition undergoes in its passage into a written form, so again we must not assume that the original tradition was in all cases uniformly good. One story may have been told less fully or less accurately than another, or the same story may have from the first taken two or more different forms. The impressions of the eyewitnesses may have varied, or the excitement of the moment may have left the memory dazed and unable to form any distinct impressions of what was seen and heard. But to discredit a narrative altogether, because it betrays imperfections such as these, is unreasonable : they are, in fact, on the whole,

---

[1] Mr. Conybeare's plea for Aristion falls short of a demonstration.
[2] *i.e.* in xxiv. 1-12, 36-53.   [3] xxiv. 13-35.

signs of veracity, for they are just the flaws which we might
expect to find in faithful reports proceeding from independent witnesses, especially if the circumstances were of
an unusual and disquieting character, and the witnesses
persons who were unaccustomed to interpret to others
the impressions left upon their own minds. The real
student will recognize that it is his duty not to reject
such evidence wholesale, but to sift it and elicit the truth
which lies at the bottom of conflicting or inadequate
testimony. If he does this with perfect honesty, he will
find that the process of sifting the Gospel narratives of
the Appearances will bring to light a great preponderance
of solid fact, which can be set aside only by the stubborn
scepticism that is born of pre-suppositions.

7. When we pass beyond the New Testament, the
echoes of the earliest tradition become few, and for the
most part untrustworthy. Even to these, however, it will
be worth our while to listen. Among the surviving
fragments of the Gospel according to the Hebrews, a
Palestinian work of the first century, there is a strange
story concerning the Lord's interview with James,[1] which
must be told in its proper place. Another fragment,
perhaps from the same Gospel,[2] relates the words of the
risen Lord at His first meeting with the Ten in a form
which differs slightly from that given by S. Luke. The
Gospel of Peter, a second century book, at the point
where our fragment comes to an abrupt end, seems to
be about to relate, with some features peculiar to itself,
the story of the meeting by the shore of the lake.[3] The

[1] Given by Jerome, *de Viris illustr.* 2.

[2] See Ignatius, *Smyrn.* 3, and Lightfoot's note.

[3] See the writer's *Akhmîm fragment of the Apocryphal Gospel of
S. Peter,* pp. 24, 28.

experience of the women at the tomb is described by a
Coptic writer of the same century in words which may
suggest that he was in part independent of the synoptists.[1]
Certain of the Oxyrhynchus sayings of Jesus, published
in recent years from fragments of papyrus found in the
valley of the Nile, may be thought to belong to the
post-Resurrection period, but the attribution is by no
means certain.[2]   No value, of course, can be attached
to such manifest romancing as we find in the so called
Testament of our Lord;[3] indeed, it may be doubted
whether the compiler intended his fiction to be regarded
as serious history.

8. The materials for our study, though drawn almost
entirely from the New Testament, are fairly abundant,
and they are trustworthy in the wider sense of the word.
But they are fragmentary; there are large gaps in our
knowledge, and the order of the facts we know is not
always certain.   In these circumstances it may be asked
whether it is wise, or even possible, to construct a con-
tinuous narrative.   While there are certain points which
can be clearly made out, others, and those not a few,
must remain tentative or conjectural.   We have no frame-
work into which we may try to fit our facts; not one
of the four Gospels presents us with a summary or an
ordered statement of the whole; S. Paul's summary, though
it is probably arranged in historical sequence, is obviously
incomplete, and was designed only to serve the purpose
of his argument.   S. Mark forsakes us almost at the first
stage; S. Matthew and S. John carry us to Galilee, and
leave us there; S. Luke does not quit Jerusalem, and

---

[1] See Harnack, in *Theol. Studien*, 1897, p. 2 ff.

[2] See Grenfell and Hunt, *New Sayings of Jesus* (1904), p. 231.

[3] See the excellent English edition by Dr. Cooper and Bp. Maclean.

in his Gospel so foreshortens the history, that he has
been thought by critics who are lacking in the sense of
humour to compress the forty days into one and place the
Ascension on the day of the Resurrection. No doubt it is
precarious to piece together narratives which are singularly
independent of each other, and the result can only be
provisional, and may be at certain points hotly disputed.
Nevertheless the attempt is worth making. In the first
place, unless it is made, it is impossible to realize the
greatness of the subject as a whole. Taken separately,
the fragments, beautiful as they are, fail to impress the
mind with the splendour of that marvellous succession
of manifestations which marked the six weeks after the
Resurrection; brought together, notwithstanding some
inevitable gaps and possible misplacements, they are seen
to be parts of the greatest revelation of the higher life
of man that the world has witnessed. Some details may
remain doubtful to the end, yet enough can be ascertained
to assure us that there is a Divine order in the manifestations of the forty days, evinced both by the purposes
which they severally fulfilled, and by the progressive
character of the teaching communicated in the sayings
of the risen Lord.

9. The visions of the ascended Christ described in the
Acts and Apocalypse are upon another plane. With one
partial exception, they were not attended by circumstances
which appealed to the senses, as the earlier appearances
did. The vision which caused the conversion of S. Paul
in some respects differs from the rest, and S. Paul himself seems to place it in the same category with the
appearances.[1] On the other hand, the visions granted to
S. Stephen and S. John were entirely in the sphere of the

---

[1] He uses ὤφθη of both alike.

seer's own mind, and presupposed an ecstatic condition in which the mind was able to realize the unseen. But the fact remains that three of the most remarkable men among the leaders of the Apostolic age believed themselves to have received revelations of Jesus Christ in His glorified state, and that one of these was at the moment when he saw the vision a determined enemy and unbeliever, and was changed by it into a devoted servant of Christ. This will not weigh heavily in favour of the truth of the Resurrection in the judgement of persons who are not convinced by the appearances of the forty days. But no one who on other grounds believes that the Lord truly rose from the dead will doubt that behind the impressions produced upon the minds of Stephen, Saul, and John there was a living Presence at work, the power of the exalted Christ ; or that through these experiences He willed to reveal to His Church so much as can now be known of the nature of His glorified life

APPEARANCES DURING THE
FORTY DAYS

*WHEN THOU HADST OVERCOME
THE SHARPNESS OF DEATH,
THOU DIDST OPEN THE KINGDOM OF HEAVEN
TO ALL BELIEVERS.*

I.

TO THE WOMEN.

AUTHORITIES: Mt. xxviii. 1-10; Mc. xvi, 1-8; 'Mc.' xvi. 9-11;
Lc. xxiv. 1-12; Jo. xx. 1-18.

AT a distance from the Cross,[1] where the Lord hung, a large[2] group of women-disciples stood and witnessed His death. Their names were known and held in honour by the Church in after years, for in Galilee they had ministered, out of their wealth or their poverty, to the wants of Jesus and the Twelve,[3] and when the time came for the last journey to Jerusalem, they had gone up with Him, and endured to the end. Among them were Mary of Magdala, out of whom the Lord had cast seven devils,[4] and another Mary, mother of two early disciples, James the Little and Joseph; Salome, the mother of the Apostles James and John, and perhaps also Joanna, the wife of Chuza, steward of Herod Antipas, and Susanna.[5]

[1] Mt. Mc. Lc. ἀπὸ μακρόθεν.   [2] Mc. ἄλλαι πολλαί.
[3] Lc. viii. 3 αὐτοῖς.   [4] Lc. l.c., 'Mc.' xvi. 9.
[5] Lc. viii. 3, xxiv. 10.

A

When all was over, the two Marys, at least,[1] lingered behind as if spellbound; and as the darkness lifted, they saw the two members of the Sanhedrin who were disciples of Jesus, Joseph from Arimathaea[2] and Nicodemus,[3] prepare the Lord's body for burial, lay it on a shelf in Joseph's new garden-tomb, which happened to be close to the place of crucifixion, and roll to the opening the great circular stone used to protect rock-tombs against intruders. Then at length the last of the women made their way back to their lodgings in the city, for darkness was approaching and the Sabbath drew on.

On the Sabbath they rested, as the Law required;[4] but after sunset, when the legal rest was over, the women[5] stole into the streets again to buy spices for the body of the dead Master. Perhaps from their distant place of observation they had not seen that it was embalmed by Joseph and Nicodemus; or, if they had, they desired to add their own tribute of devotion.

That night, it may be believed, they slept little; and before daybreak[6] on the first day of the week

---

[1] Mt., Mc.; cf. Lc.　　　　[2] Mt., Mc., Lc.　　　[3] Jo. xix. 39 ff.
[4] Lc. xxiii. 56.　　　　　　[5] Mc. includes Salome.

[6] Mt. τῇ ἐπιφωσκούσῃ, Mc. λίαν πρωί, Lc. ὄρθρου βαθέως, Jo. σκοτίας ἔτι οὔσης. Mt.'s ὀψὲ σαββάτων and Mc.'s ἀνατείλαντος (v.l. ἀνατέλλοντος) τοῦ ἡλίου can hardly be pressed in view of this consensus.

they were on their way to Joseph's garden. Our first Gospel, which reports that on the day after the Crucifixion the tomb had been sealed and guarded by Pilate's soldiers at the desire of the Sanhedrin, supposes that their purpose was to gaze at the tomb again from a safe distance ; but the older narrative of S. Mark says plainly that they went with the intention of anointing the body.[1] Plainly they knew nothing of the sealing or the watch, and it was not until they were well on their way that it occurred to them to ask how the great stone, which they had seen rolled to the door, was to be removed.[2] A gloss in one of the MSS. of S. Luke says that twenty men could hardly have rolled it away [3]—an exaggeration, of course ; but it would certainly have defied the strength of a few women. The difficulty, however, melted away almost as soon as it was realized : they were now in view of the tomb, and in the growing light of the dawn they could see that the stone had been pushed aside. Here the first Gospel again interposes a statement which is not in the others : there had been a great earthquake, which had

---

[1] Mt. θεωρῆσαι τὸν τάφον, Mc. ἵνα . . . ἀλείψωσιν αὐτόν.

[2] The apocryphal Peter-Gospel suggests that if unable to carry out their purpose, they intended to lay what they brought at the door of the tomb (§ 11 κἂν ἐπὶ τῆς θύρας βάλωμεν ἃ φέρομεν).

[3] ὃν μόγις εἴκοσι ἐκύλιον (cod. D).

rolled it away. In any case the women, whose simple story is given by S. Mark, did not stop to inquire the cause of the stone's removal. The sight of the open tomb quickened their steps; and presently they were pushing their way in, when they were startled by a bright light inside. Afterwards, when they came to tell their tale, impressions were found to differ; one thought she saw a white-robed youth sitting on the right of the entrance; another reported that two men in dazzling attire appeared to them.[1] A third story was that an angel of the Lord[2] had rolled away the stone, paralysing with fear the soldiers who were watching the tomb, and that it was he who now shewed himself to the women on their arrival at the tomb.

What happened cannot now be determined exactly, but some startling phenomena must lie behind these independent accounts. The women were dumb with fear,[3] whereupon a voice bade them fear not; they were seeking Jesus who had been crucified; He was not in the tomb; He had risen, He was alive; let them go with speed and tell His disciples, and Peter in particular,[4] that He was risen, and was going in advance of

[1] Mc. νεανίσκον καθήμενον. Lc. ἄνδρες δύο ἐπέστησαν αὐταῖς.

[2] Mt. ἄγγελος Κυρίου.   [3] Mc. ἐξεθαμβήθησαν.

[4] Mc. καὶ τῷ Πέτρῳ.

them into Galilee, where they would see Him as He had promised.[1]

One of the party, as it appears, did not see the vision of angels or hear their message. At the first glance, which shewed that the tomb was empty, or perhaps as soon as she realized that it was open, Mary of Magdala had hastened back to the city,[2] to seek Peter, the first of the Apostles, and John, the disciple whom Jesus had loved, and with whom His mother now was.[3] The Magdalene's tale roused the two men from their stupor; here was indeed a new turn in the course of events, under which they could not sit still. They ran together to the tomb to see for themselves what had happened ; and John, arriving first, was satisfied by one eager look that the body was gone,[4] since the linen wraps were lying where it had been. Peter, who followed, with characteristic promptness entered the cave, and noted further that the head-cloth had been separated from the rest of the linen, and rolled up[5] by itself, doubt-

[1] Mc. καθὼς εἶπεν ὑμῖν: cf. Mt. καθὼς εἶπεν. Lc. has quite another version of the words (xxiv. 5-7).

[2] Jo. xx. 1 ff.   [3] Jo. xix. 27.

[4] Sanday, *Criticism of the Fourth Gospel*, p. 91 : 'He is fleet of foot and outstrips his companion, but he is also of a finer and more sensitive mould, and when he reaches the tomb a feeling of awe comes over him and he pauses for a moment outside.'

[5] ἐντετυλιγμένον.

less at the raised end of the chamber where the head rested.[1] Then John also went in, and saw what Peter had seen; and, as he afterwards remembered, he believed;[2] there arose in his mind at that moment a nascent confidence that in some way as yet unknown their darkness would be turned to light, and the victory of the Christ be secured. For the present, however, the mystery remained unsolved; they seemed to have exhausted their means of getting at the truth, and both men went home again.

But Mary, who had followed them to the tomb, was not satisfied. When they were gone, after John's example, she looked into the tomb, and at once she saw what even he had missed: a vision of white angels sitting, one at the head, the other at the feet, where the Lord's body had lain. Was it only the glint of the linen body-clothes and head-dress? Or was it indeed a spiritual reality, which could be seen only in an ecstasy? A voice from within the tomb came to her, which asked why she wept; and without fear or any

[1] See Latham, *Risen Master*, plate 2, for an imaginary sketch of the interior.

[2] εἶδεν καὶ ἐπίστευσεν. 'It is not likely that it [ἐπίστευσεν] means simply "believed that the body had been removed," as Mary Magdalene reported' (Westcott). 'That rising faith John kept to himself . . . perhaps his first public mention of it was when, so many years afterwards, he sat down to write that Gospel which bears his name' (Hanna, *The Forty Days*, p. 31).

token of surprise she answered in the words of which her mind was full: [1] *They have taken away my Lord, and I know not where they have laid him.* Then, turning away from the tomb, she found herself face to face with a man in the dress of working life. Her eyes were dim with tears, and she did not recognize him; but the thought flashed into her mind that it was Joseph's gardener, and that his presence explained everything; doubtless it was he who, on returning to work after the Sabbath, had rolled back the stone and removed the body. She begs him to let her know where it is,[2] and she will remove it out of his way.

In the greatest moments of life words are few. Jesus said 'Mary'; she, 'Master.'[3] *The good shepherd calleth his own sheep by name, . . . and the sheep follow him, for they know his voice.*[4] Mary was seized by an irresistible desire to grasp what she had found, to convince herself that it was not a vision only, to detain the Lord lest He

---

[1] Nearly the same words had been said by her to Peter and John (*v.* 2).

[2] 'Her heart is so full of the Person . . . that she assumes that He is known to her questioner' (Westcott).

[3] The Aramaic word (*Rabbuni*) is given.

[4] Cf. Latham, *Risen Master*, p. 235: 'It is so exactly after our Lord's manner that He should recall her to a knowledge of Him by uttering her name, that I see an assurance of veritable historical relation here.'

should be taken from her again. But the risen Christ checks the impulse : *Touch me not, for I am not yet ascended unto the Father ; but go unto my brethren and say to them, I ascend unto my Father and your Father, and to my God and your God.* It seems at first sight a strange answer to the loyalty of the most loyal of disciples, at the very moment of reunion. There must have been a stern necessity for such an apparent repulse. It was necessary to make it clear at once that old relations were not to be restored, as Mary evidently hoped ; that the Resurrection was the beginning of a new order. The Lord's " Touch me not " does not mean that the risen body was intangible, for it was afterwards offered to the touch of all the Apostles ; [1] nor is it a refusal of intercourse of any kind with disciples who are still in the flesh. On the contrary, the words that follow imply that the intimacy of the life in Galilee is to be exchanged for a new fellowship of a closer kind.[2] The Resurrection must, however, first be consummated by the Ascension ; the visible presence must be finally withdrawn before the presence of Jesus in the Spirit can be realized.[3]

---

[1] Lc. xxiv. 39 ψηλαφήσατέ με, Jo. xx. 27.

[2] μή μου ἅπτου, οὔπω γὰρ ἀναβέβηκα.

[3] Cyril of Alexandria : τουτέστιν, οὔπω τὸ ἅγιον πνεῦμα κατέπεμψα πρὸς ὑμᾶς. He compares Jo. xvi. 7.

The first saying of the risen Lord is therefore at once a warning against a mistaken hope, and a promise of something higher than that which is to be withdrawn. These brief appearances are presently to be superseded by a life of fellowship which on His side will be unbroken ; the spiritual and eternal is to take the place of the visible and temporal.[1] If Mary may not hold the prize which she thinks that she has won, it is only because to keep it would be to lose one immeasurably greater. Meanwhile, it is her privilege to carry to the Lord's brethren the first tidings of the Resurrection and incipient Ascension,[2] and with it a new assurance that His Father was their Father, and His God their God, with all the great hopes which such an announcement must create.

Mary, unable to detain the Master, hastened back to Jerusalem to deliver her message. She found the disciples in the depth of despair,[3] for by this time they all knew that the worst had happened : the body of the Master was missing. We can see her break into the gloomy gathering with the excited

[1] For the theology of this great saying see Bp. Moberly, *Sayings of the great Forty Days*, p. 82 ff.

[2] οὔπω ἀναβέβηκα, yet ἀναβαίνω. The withdrawal from the visible world and exaltation to 'heaven' began in fact from the moment of the Resurrection.

[3] 'Mc.' πενθοῦσι καὶ κλαίουσιν.

cry, 'The Lord is alive; I have seen Him, He has spoken[1] to me; He has bidden me tell you that He is about to ascend to God.'[2]   But her words, it seems, awakened no response.[3]   Hope was dead within these men; it was not to be roused by the ravings of a half-frantic woman.   So far was Mary of Magdala from creating the belief in the Lord's resurrection,[4] that for hours, as it appears, she alone believed; or if there were others who shared her conviction, they were not to be found among the Apostles or the men of their company.[5]

We left the other women of Mary's party at the moment when the angel at the tomb entrusted them with a message for the Eleven.   But they scarcely waited to hear it   The dazzling vision, the voice from the grave, filled them with dismay; they turned and fled, and on their way back to the city, so great was their terror, not a word was spoken, not a greeting exchanged with a passing friend; *they said nothing to any one; for they were afraid.* Here the genuine S. Mark comes to an abrupt end. If, as may be inferred from the first and third

[1] Jo. ἑώρακα . . . εἶπεν.   Cf. 'Mc.' ζῇ καὶ ἐθεάθη.

[2] v. 18.   [3] 'Mc.' ἠπίστησαν.

[4] Renan, *Vie de Jésus*, p. 450: 'La passion d'une hallucinée donne au monde un Dieu ressuscité.' Cf. *Les Apôtres*, p. 13.

[5] Cf. Lc. xxiv. 11, which probably describes the effect of the words of Mary as well as of the other women. 'Mc.' xvi. 14 is another reminiscence of the same fact.

Gospels,[1] the women ultimately delivered their message, it was received by the Apostles with disbelief, even with scorn ; *these words appeared in their sight as idle talk*,[2] unworthy of serious consideration.

S. Matthew adds that on their way to the Eleven the other women were met, as Mary had been, by the risen Lord. He greeted them with the salutation of ordinary life ;[3] they, recognizing Him at once, fell at His feet and clasped them, unrebuked.[4] He bade them not to fear, and repeated the angel's message : *go tell my brethren that they depart into Galilee, and there shall they see me.* Notwithstanding the manifest differences between the details of this story and those of the appearance to Mary, it may reasonably be doubted whether the two narratives do not relate to the same incident. In the first and third Gospels there certainly seems to be some confusion between Mary's return to Jerusalem

[1] Mt. xxviii. 16 seems to presuppose that the Eleven received the message of *v.* 7 ; Lc. xxiv. 9 says expressly that the women reported what they had heard, though Lc.'s account of the angel's words differs.

[2] ὡσεὶ λῆρος.

[3] χαίρετε, the Greek salutation, as 'peace' was the salutation of the Semitic East : cf. Lc. i. 28. This is perhaps obscured by the 'All hail' of the English versions, which from long associations suggests a greeting peculiarly solemn and perhaps of mystical import.

[4] There was no need to repeat the lesson which had been taught to the Magdalene ; or perhaps the other women were not ready to receive it.

and the return of the other women, and it is possible that the first Gospel has worked into the latter some features of the interview which belong to the former. It is not surprising if, with the exception of the evidently genuine reminiscences in the fourth Gospel, the story of the women has reached us in a less certain form than the rest of the narratives of the forty days. The first surprises of the Resurrection Day fell to the share of witnesses who were little qualified to retain or to communicate to others an exact and connected account of what they saw and heard. It was natural, moreover, that less importance should be attached to their story than to the accounts of the later appearances; the appearance to the women was superseded, as it seemed, by the abundant manifestations of the risen Christ which followed. In these circumstances the uncertainties which attend the Synoptic accounts of the doings of the women at the tomb are not greater than we might have expected, and cast no shadow of suspicion on the general truth of the narrative.

II.

TO SIMON PETER.

AUTHORITIES: Lc. xxiv. 34; 1 Cor. xv. 5.

IF Mary of Magdala was the leader of the women-disciples of the Lord,[1] Simon Peter was yet more decidedly foremost among the men, both in office and by force of character. He stands first in all lists of the Twelve, the most conspicuous person in the first group of Apostles.[2] He possessed a nature at once impetuous and strenuous; if James and John were 'sons of thunder,' Simon was 'the rock,' on whose rugged strength the storms of life would beat to little purpose, who might be trusted to rise again and again out of the waves that went over him.

But on the morning of the Resurrection he was for the moment in the lowest depths. There was

---

[1] As her place in all the narratives seems to intimate. In the Coptic Gnostic literature edited by Schmidt (*Texte u. Unters.* viii.) this priority of the Magdalene is pressed in an exaggerated way: see Schmidt, p. 452 ff.

[2] Mt. x. 2 πρῶτος Σίμων.

no sadder man in Jerusalem. In common with his brethren, he had lost the Master ; even His dead body had now been taken from them. But Peter had also a private grief, and one of his own making. The bitter weeping which followed the denial had left his heart sore and angry with itself. Since Friday morning he had been brooding, perhaps in the silence of a solitary lodging, over the irretrievable past and the hopeless future. It had been almost a relief when Mary brought word that the tomb was empty, for the tidings was a call to action ; it broke for a time the monotony of his gloomy thoughts to hasten with John to the garden outside the walls, to examine the tomb, and form his own conclusions. But whereas in the mind of John a new faith seems to have sprung up at the sight of the separated and folded linen, Simon Peter went back as he came. The day wore on, the strain became intolerable, and he left the house again to seek rest from his burden. Perhaps he retraced his steps to the tomb in the hope of gaining further light ; perhaps he sought comfort in the memories awakened by Gethsemane, the mount of Olives, the village of Bethany. On the way the Lord appeared to him, as He had appeared to Mary when she turned from the empty tomb. For this fact we have a guarantee which is scarcely open to dispute. When, eight or nine

years after the first Easter day, Saul went up to
Jerusalem 'to visit Cephas,'[1] who can doubt that
the conversation turned upon the appearances of the
risen Lord ; or that while Saul had much to say
of his experiences on the Damascus road, S. Peter
told how the Master had appeared to himself on
the very day of the Resurrection ? ' He appeared
to Cephas' was thenceforth a prominent feature in
the Gospel which S. Paul delivered to the Gentile
churches.[2] Yet nothing more than the bare fact
has reached us, and what passed between the Lord
and His disciple it would be worse than idle to
conjecture. The words of Christ, more especially
of the risen Christ, are marked by their unexpected-
ness ; though for the most part they arise out of
some passing incident, they are seldom obvious ;
it is only upon reflection that we realize their
perfect appositeness, their inexhaustible fulness.
The words spoken by the Lord on this occasion [3]
were probably not divulged by S. Peter ; he kept
them locked up in his own mind as a sacred
treasure. He had not been entrusted, like Mary,
with a message for the Church ; the Lord's words
to him were meant only for himself. Therefore

---

[1] Gal. i. 18 ἱστορῆσαι Κηφᾶν.

[2] 1 Cor. xv. 3 ff. Cf. p. xii. note 3.

[3] For those spoken to him before others on the later occasion
see p. 59 ff.

they did not enter into his preaching, and had no place, we may be fairly sure, in the lost ending of S. Mark, or in the collection of sayings which was used by the authors of our first and third Gospels ; they were not communicated even to S. Paul.   But while the words themselves died with S. Peter, and their precise nature cannot even be conjectured, it is permissible to believe that they combined in the Master's inimitable way the tenderness and the sternness [1] of a Divine love, and that they completed the conversion of the penitent Apostle, restoring his peace of mind, and enabling him to stablish his brethren.[2]

Although it was Mary who for her greater loyalty was counted worthy to see the risen Lord first, it was not Mary's report, as Renan supposes, that let in the first ray of hope upon the disciples, but Simon Peter's.   Later in the day the Eleven and their company were found radiant with the conviction that the Lord had risen indeed, since He had appeared to Simon.[3]   The Apostle who had risen from his fall through the words of absolution that came from the risen Christ was the first to bring the Gospel of the Resurrection home to the hearts of his fellows.

[1] Rom. xi. 22 ἴδε οὖν χρηστότητα καὶ ἀποτομίαν θεοῦ.

[2] Lc. xxii. 32 σύ ποτε ἐπιστρέψας στήρισον τοὺς ἀδελφούς σου.

[3] Lc. xxiv. 34.

III.

TO CLEOPAS AND ANOTHER.

AUTHORITIES: 'Mc.' xvi. 12, 13; Lc. xxiv. 13-35.

BEFORE Peter had returned to the company, two of the men-disciples had occasion to set out for a village some miles distant from the city. It was Emmaus, not Emmaus Nicopolis, the modern Amwâs, which is twenty miles off, but either the present Kalôniyeh, close to the ruins of Joshua's Mozah,[1] or el Kubêbeh, a little further to the north-west.[2] Of the travellers one was a certain Cleopas or Cleopatros, whose Greek name has suggested a connexion with the court of Herod;[3] the other is unknown, but neither of the two belonged to the number of the Eleven.[4]

As they crossed the hills which descend from Jerusalem to the Mediterranean, the men conversed[5]

[1] Josh. xviii. 26.

[2] See Dr. Sanday's *Sacred Sites*, p. 29 ff. and plate xxviii.

[3] Hastings, *D.B.* ii. 639ᵃ.   [4] Cf. Lc. xxiv. 33.

[5] The Joppa road would allow of their walking side by side: see Latham, *R.M.* p. 103 f.

B

on the topic of which their hearts were full. An eager discussion arose between them,[1] perhaps as to the credibility of the story told by the women, and they did not notice the approach of one who was gaining upon them from behind. Presently he overtook the two, and stood by their side; and in their surprise they stopped short on their way,[2] as though inviting the stranger to join them. He noticed the settled gloom on their faces,[3] and asked what they were so keenly debating. Cleopas answered that he must surely be some solitary sojourner[4] in Jerusalem if he was ignorant of the events of the last few days. The other simply asked what kind[5] of events Cleopas meant. His reply is instructive, for it reveals the thoughts which were passing in the minds of the rank and file of the disciples. A mighty prophet, he said, a prophet to whom they had looked to ransom[6] Israel, had been delivered over to the Romans by the heads of the nation, and put to death by crucifixion; and this tragedy had been enacted three days ago. This morning, however, strange reports had reached them; some women of the party,[7] who had gone

---

[1] Lc. ἐν τῷ . . . συνζητεῖν: οἱ λόγοι οὗτοι οὓς ἀντιβάλλετε.

[2] ἐστάθησαν.

[3] σκυθρωποί. Latham illustrates this by imagining a pair of Royalists going on foot out of London on Jan. 30, 1649.

[4] σὺ μόνος παροικεῖς; or, 'the only sojourner.'

[5] ποῖα;   [6] λυτροῦσθαι.   [7] ἐξ ἡμῶν.

to the tomb at daybreak, brought tidings that the body was not there, and that they had been told by angels that Jesus was alive ; moreover, the disappearance of the body was confirmed by members of their own company [1] who had been to see for themselves.

One can see the perplexity which filled the minds of these Galilean or Judaean [2] disciples. They knew not what to believe. On the one hand there was no doubt that the Master was a prophet, and a great prophet ; both His words and His mighty works had shewn Him to be this, and nothing that befell Him could efface the impression produced by His ministry. But was He also, as they had fondly hoped, the Christ ? Where was now their dream of national deliverance under His leadership ? What did the crucifixion, the burial, the three days spent in the tomb, mean but the total failure of these hopes ? And yet, what was to be thought of the women's story, partly confirmed by two such men as Peter and John ?

The reply of the stranger is not reported at length, but Cleopas remembered afterwards the stinging reproof with which it began. ' *Foolish*

[1] τινές τῶν σὺν ἡμῖν.

[2] Mr. Latham gives reasons for preferring the latter supposition ; see *Risen Master*, p. 199 ff.

men, and slow of heart,[1] you have never really believed the prophets which have been read in your ears every Sabbath day. Had you understood their teaching, you would see that all has happened as they said it must happen. There was a moral necessity[2] that the Christ should suffer before He reigned; that He should redeem by suffering, and not by a forcible repression of evil.' Then, as Cleopas further recollected, the rest of the way was beguiled with a fascinating study of the old Scriptures; one after another they were unlocked, as with the key of David, and laid open before the two disciples; and, as the great Expositor passed from Moses to Malachi,[3] there rose up before them the picture of the suffering, conquering Christ, until their hearts glowed with the fire[4] of a new hope. Who was this companion of their road? Could it be indeed—but no, the thought was incredible, they must put it from them.

When they reached Emmaus the sun was low in the west,[5] and the Mediterranean already aglow

---

[1] ὦ ἀνόητοι καὶ βραδεῖς τῇ καρδίᾳ. For similar reproofs cf. Mc. vii. 18, viii. 17, 'xvi.' 14.

[2] δεῖ.

[3] On the loss of these and similar utterances see some good remarks in Latham p. 118 f.

[4] οὐχὶ ἡ καρδία ἡμῶν καιομένη ἦν;

[5] κέκλικεν ἤδη ἡ ἡμέρα.

with the last brightness of daylight. Their companion, it seemed, had further to go ; perhaps his
destination was Lydda, or even Joppa. But when
urged to spend the night with them he yielded,[1]
and entered the house where the two were staying—whether it was an inn or the home of one
of them, we do not know. The simple meal was
soon prepared, and the three reclined at the table.
Before them, with other food, were cakes of
unleavened bread, baked for the Passover week.
The stranger, as if he were the host, took one of
the loaves,[2] and pronouncing the customary benediction, broke it into two or three pieces and
gave one to each of them. It was the Lord ; they
knew Him now. The next moment His place
was empty, He had vanished out of their sight.[3]
But His purpose had been fulfilled ; He had opened
their minds to understand, and their eyes to recognize Him. They knew now that the Messiah was
destined to die and to rise again ; they knew
also that Jesus was the Messiah, and that He
had indeed risen from the dead.

Why had they not known Him before ? S. Luke
explains that their eyes had been *holden, that they*

---

[1] παρεβιάσαντο.   [2] τὸν ἄρτον.

[3] ἄφαντος ἐγένετο ἀπ' αὐτῶν. The words speak of a disappearance
only, not a local withdrawal.   Mr. Latham (p. 144) well disposes of
Renan's attempt to account for the sudden departure, as he conceives
it (*Les Apôtres*, p. 20).

should not know him. The appendix to S. Mark
says that He *was manifested in another form,*[1] which
may mean either that He did not look as when He
was with them before the Passion—some change
had passed over His appearance and possibly His
dress—or, if the words were originally preceded
by an account of the appearance to Mary, there
may be a reference in them to her impression that
He was the gardener; to the two on the way to
Emmaus He wore another aspect, not that of the
labourer at his work, but rather of the traveller
with his loins girded, shoes on his feet, a staff in
his hand.   But however this may have been,
doubtless the ultimate reason why the two did not
know Him was that, as S. Luke says, their eyes were
spellbound.[2]   Either they did not suspect that the
stranger was Jesus, or if the suspicion crossed their
minds, it was promptly dismissed.   There is nothing
psychologically impossible in such a situation, if
the men were still possessed by the conviction that,
in spite of what they had heard, the Lord was
still among the dead.   It is less easy to under-

---

[1] ἐν ἑτέρᾳ μορφῇ. It was not, however, such a μεταμόρφωσις as
He underwent on the mount (Mc. ix. 2). When Professor Harnack
(*What is Christianity?* p. 161) speaks of the risen Christ as ' so
glorified that His own could not immediately recognize him,' he
reads into the Gospel narratives what is not there. There is no
trace of any such transfiguration during the forty days.

[2] ἐκρατοῦντο.

stand how they failed to recognize the voice, or to feel that no other man was capable of opening the Scriptures as He had done. It must be remembered, however, that, so far as we know, expositions of this kind had no place in Christ's pre-resurrection teaching; and further, that these two men, who were not Apostles, may never before have come into close quarters with the Master. Besides all this, with our ignorance of the conditions of the risen body, we cannot assume that either look or voice were altogether such as they had been in mortal life, or indeed that they were always the same during the forty days.

Another question arises from this story. How is the sudden disappearance of the Lord's body to be explained? Everything else in the narrative goes to show that the body was not 'docetic,' but real : a body constituted like our own. The Lord walked side by side with the two disciples for some miles; He had spoken at great length; He had entered a house, had reclined at table, had taken, broken, and distributed bread. All these are the acts of one who possessed a material human frame; yet in an instant His body becomes invisible, as if it had never been more than an apparition. Other evidence of the same kind will come before us as we proceed, but as this is the first instance, it may be well to consider the point

once for all. In the first place, it would seem
that even in His mortal state the Lord possessed
some peculiar power of withdrawing His visible
presence when He desired to do so. At Nazareth,
when the townsfolk sought to throw Him over a
precipice, *passing through the midst of them he
went his way.*[1] After the miracle at Bethesda[2]
Jesus conveyed himself away,[3] *a multitude being in
the place.* When in the Temple-court the Jews
took up stones to cast at Him,[4] *he hid himself,*[5]
and went out of the Temple. Such instances suggest
that before the Passion the Lord's sinless human
will possessed a power over His body which is
wholly beyond our experience or comprehension.
Of the conditions to which His risen body was
subject we know nothing, but it may well have
been yet more completely under the control of the
will. No presumption, then, against the reality of
the Resurrection can fairly be based on the statement that the risen Christ made Himself visible
or invisible at pleasure. Further, in judging of
His use of such a power, it is necessary to remember
the twofold purpose which He seems to have had
in view. On the one hand He willed to demonstrate
both the truth of the Resurrection and the identity
of the person who rose with Jesus who was

[1] Lc. iv. 30.   [2] Jo. v. 13.   [3] ἐξένευσεν.
[4] Jo. viii. 59.   [5] ἐκρύβη.

crucified ; on the other, it was no less important
to prepare His disciples during the short space of
six weeks for His final withdrawal from visibility.
Hence these alternations of appearance and disappearance, of a visible presence and an invisible.
The Emmaus incident illustrates the law which
governed these. The Lord remained visible to the
two disciples just long enough to remove the last
doubt of His identity, and then, as the old familiar
intercourse was about to be resumed, He withdrew
Himself from their eyes, and they learnt the truth,
not less needful for them to learn, that He
belonged to a new order, and that the claims of
the invisible world were upon Him, a world into
which they could not follow Him as yet.

IV.

TO THE TEN AND OTHERS.

AUTHORITIES: Lc. xxiv. 36-43; Jo. xx. 19-21; 1 Cor. xv. 5; Ignatius, *Smyrn.* 3.

WHEN the Lord vanished out of the sight of the two disciples at Emmaus, as soon as the first surprise was over,[1] they girded themselves for another journey, and retraced their steps to Jerusalem. Whatever the business may have been that called them to Emmaus, it was of no account in comparison with the duty of reporting their great experience to the Eleven without delay.[2] As Mary of Magdala had hastened from the empty tomb to the lodging of Peter and John, so the two now made their way to the room where at this hour the whole company[3] would be assembled for the evening meal.[4] They reached the place big with tidings

[1] Lc. αὐτῇ τῇ ὥρᾳ.

[2] Their loyalty was rewarded by witnessing the yet greater manifestation which was to follow: see Latham, *Risen Master*, p. 153 f.

[3] Lc. τοὺς ἕνδεκα καὶ τοὺς σὺν αὐτοῖς.

[4] 'Mc.' ἀνακειμένοις.

which they believed themselves the first to bring. But they had been forestalled. When the door was unbarred they were greeted at once with the cry, *The Lord is risen indeed, and hath appeared to Simon*.[1] Yet the joy, the amazement of the Eleven and their party must have grown sensibly as the two told their story, with the fulness of the Eastern love of detail [2]—how the Stranger overtook them on the road, what He said, how He 'opened the Scriptures,' how in the end He was revealed to them, and then at once disappeared.[3]

It was now evening, and save for the moonlight, dark ; the sun had been low in the heavens when they reached Emmaus, nearly two hours ago.[4] The door of the chamber had been barred again after the admission of the two brethren, to make sure against a sudden attack by the emissaries of the Sanhedrin ; for the disciples were still haunted by the fear of attack.[5] Suddenly, while the two were

---

[1] Cf. p. 14 ff. Of the Evangelists S. Luke alone, as we might have expected, shares S. Paul's knowledge of the appearance to S. Peter.

[2] Lc. ἐξηγοῦντο τὰ ἐν τῇ ὁδῷ κτλ.

[3] 'Mc.'s' οὐδὲ ἐκείνοις ἐπίστευσαν is either from a later and less accurate account, or it must be taken to refer to some who still held out against the growing evidence of the Resurrection.

[4] Doubtless, as Mr. Latham acutely says (p. 124), they walked 'in the rapid way people do who have great news to carry.' Still the distance could hardly be covered in less than the time stated.

[5] Jo. διὰ τὸν φόβον τῶν Ἰουδαίων.

yet describing what had passed between themselves
and the risen Christ,[1] they became conscious of a
Presence in their midst : a form was seen standing
before them ; a voice greeted them with the customary, ' Peace be unto you.'   In an instant their
joy changed to terror ; they believed themselves to
have seen a spirit.   A year ago in Galilee, when He
came to them walking on the sea, they had cried
out with fear, exclaiming, ' It is an apparition.'[2]
The same panic seized them now ; the form which
had broken in upon their securely-barred retreat
could only be a phantom, not a living man.[3]   To
reassure them, it was not enough to say, as on the
former occasion, *It is I ; be not afraid*, for they
knew that He had been among the dead, and would
need proof that He was indeed risen again.   So
the Lord gave them this also.   *Why are ye troubled?*
He asks, *and wherefore do reasonings arise in your
heart ?   See my hands and my feet, that it is I
myself.*   So saying, He shewed them the hands
and feet that had been pierced by the nails of the
Cross, and the side into which the soldier's lance
had been driven ;[4] He offered them to their touch.
Take, handle me, one report of the words makes

---

[1] Lc. ταῦτα δὲ αὐτῶν λαλούντων.   [2] Mt. xiv. 26 φάντασμά ἐστιν.

[3] Lc. ἐδόκουν πνεῦμα (cod. D, φάντασμα) θεωρεῖν.

[4] Lc. ἴδετε τὰς χεῖράς μου καὶ τοὺς πόδας μου. Jo. ἔδειξεν καὶ τὰς
χεῖρας καὶ τὴν πλευρὰν αὐτοῖς.

Him say, *and see that I am not a bodiless spirit*;[1] *handle me and see*, S. Luke puts it, *for a spirit hath not flesh and bones as ye behold me having*. When their very joy kept them from believing Him,[2] He ate before them some of the fried fish[3] which remained from their evening meal. It was clear at length to the dullest comprehension that His body was not docetic but real, and that it was the body which had been crucified. His saying had been fulfilled, *Where two or three are gathered together in my name, there am I in the midst of them.*[4]

The joy of that moment was long remembered. *The disciples were glad when they saw the Lord*; so at the end of the century the beloved disciple wrote with the memory of that first vision of the risen Christ still fresh in his mind. If we may trust the writer of the appendix to S. Mark, there was that which sobered their joy at the time, for the Lord at once reproached[5] the Eleven for the

---

[1] Ignatius, *Letter to the Smyrnaeans*, 3 λάβετε, ψηλαφήσατέ με, καὶ ἴδετε ὅτι οὐκ εἰμὶ δαιμόνιον ἀσώματον. This came, according to Jerome, from the Gospel according to the Hebrews; according to Origen, from the Doctrine of Peter.

[2] Lc. ἀπιστούντων αὐτῶν ἀπὸ τῆς χαρᾶς.

[3] The inferior MSS. add 'and of a honeycomb.'

[4] Mt. xviii. 20.

[5] 'Mc.' xvi. 14 ὠνείδισεν τὴν ἀπιστίαν αὐτῶν. Neither S. Luke nor S. John shews any knowledge of this, and it may be that the later writer has confused the occasion with that described in Lc. xxiv. 25.

unbelief which had led them to reject the witness
of the women who saw Him in the early hours of
the day.   But if this reproof was judged necessary
by a love which does not shrink from inflicting
salutary pain, it was soon succeeded by words that
healed the wound.   The Lord, S. John tells us,[1]
repeated His *Peace be unto you.*   With Him the
words of greeting were no empty formality.   Before
the Passion He said, *Not as the world giveth
give I unto you;*[2] and the Resurrection imparted
a yet deeper meaning to His ' peace.'   The Resurrection was a divine assurance that peace had been
re-established between God and His world ; and
the original disciples of the Lord, who had ' continued with Him in His temptations,'[3] were the
first to receive the message of this reconciliation,[4]
as they were to be the first to publish it to
mankind.   For the great tasks which lay before
them He now proceeded to give them the necessary
powers.

As the Father hath sent me, even so send I you.[5]
Jesus Himself had been sent, entrusted with a
mission, and one which none but Himself could

---

[1] $\epsilon\hat{\iota}\pi\epsilon\nu$ . . . $\pi\acute{a}\lambda\iota\nu$. Augustine : ' iteratio confirmatio est.'

[2] Jo. xiv. 27.   [3] Lc. xxii. 28.

[4] 2 Cor. v. 19 $\tau\grave{o}\nu$ $\lambda\acute{o}\gamma o\nu$ $\tau\hat{\eta}s$ $\kappa a\tau a\lambda\lambda a\gamma\hat{\eta}s$.

[5] $\kappa a\theta\grave{\omega}s$ $\dot{a}\pi\acute{\epsilon}\sigma\tau a\lambda\kappa\acute{\epsilon}\nu$ $\mu\epsilon$ $\dot{o}$ $\pi a\tau\acute{\eta}\rho$, $\kappa\dot{a}\gamma\grave{\omega}$ $\pi\acute{\epsilon}\mu\pi\omega$ $\dot{\upsilon}\mu\hat{a}s$. The variations
of verb and tense are to be noted.

fulfil. He was the Apostle,[1] the Representative of
the Father. Of this mission of Jesus the fourth
Gospel is specially full,[2] though like other ideas which
are labelled as ' Johannine,' it comes to the surface
now and again in the Synoptic Gospels.[3] The
Lord's mission had occupied a prominent place in
that last prayer, the echoes of which must still
have been ringing in the ears of the Eleven.[4]
But now He had finished the work which the
Father had given Him to do on earth in His
own person ; henceforth He would work through
others. Early in the ministry He had sent forth
twelve whom He called His Apostles,[5] His delegates
even as He was the Father's Delegate. Was He
now merely renewing a commission which He
had given before ? No doubt He renewed it, but
in doing so He made it wider and permanent.
The new commission is wider, for it is not limited
to the Apostolate ; the other disciples who were
present are included, and with the Eleven they
represent the whole Church. And it is permanent ;
for while the Apostolate was temporary, the Church
as a whole lives on to the end, and as long as she

[1] Heb. iii. 1.

[2] See Jo. iii. 17, 34 ; v. 36, 38 ; vi. 29, 57 ; vii. 29 ; viii. 42 ; x.
36 ; xi. 42.

[3] *e.g.* in Mc. ix. 37, xii. 6.   [4] Jo. xvii. 3, 23.

[5] Mc. iii. 14 οὓς καὶ ἀποστόλους ὠνόμασεν.

lives she retains the missionary character impressed
upon her by the risen Lord. At the same time
His first saying, at least as it is seen in S. John's
idealistic rendering, places once for all the permanent mission of the Church in its true relation to
the mission of Jesus Christ. The mission of the
Church is not a separate or independent task, but
one which is altogether secondary and subordinate,
resting upon, flowing out of, the Divine mission
of her Lord.[1] His mission was not exhausted by
His earthly ministry, His death, or even His
victory over death ; but henceforth it fulfils itself
in the subordinate mission of the Christian society
acting in His name and by His Spirit.

The risen Lord, Himself sent into the world
by the Father, now in His turn sends His Church.
But He does not send her unequipped. He had
been conceived by the Holy Spirit and, before
the ministry, baptized with the Spirit ; in the power
of the Spirit [2] He had entered on the work which
had now been accomplished. If the Church was
to carry on His mission, she also must be born
of the Spirit, baptized with the Spirit, inspired
by the Spirit, and thus enabled to do her part
in the regeneration of the world. Hence the

---

[1] On S. John's use of ἀποστέλλειν and πέμπειν see the additional
note in Westcott's *Commentary on S. John.*

[2] Lc. iv. 14.

Lord's next act, after the solemn sending, was to endow those whom He sent with His own Spirit. *He breathed on them and saith unto them, Receive the Holy Ghost.*

More than once S. John's Gospel carries its reader back to the beginnings of the world and of our race. *In the beginning was the Word*, reminds us of Gen. i. 1 ; *He breathed on them*, of Gen. ii. 7, *The Lord God formed man of the dust of the ground, and breathed into his nostrils the breath of life, and man became a living soul.*[1] The beloved disciple, it may be inferred, wishes to teach that this breathing on the part of the risen Christ is analogous to the Divine breathing which inspired human nature with a life higher than that of the mere animal.[2] The first Adam was made by the Breath of God a living soul ; the last Adam, the Lord from heaven, became by His resurrection a life-giving spirit, able to breathe into His fellow-men the very breath of life.[3] Of the exercise of this new prerogative the act of breathing on the assembly was the outward, visible sign ; the sacrament of an inward, spiritual quickening. The coming of the Holy Spirit, the Breath

[1] S. John uses in *c.* xx. 22 the verb which the LXX use in Gen. ii. 7 (ἐνεφύσησεν). See also Ezek. xxxvii. 9 (LXX).

[2] Cf. Driver in *Westminster Commentaries*, Genesis, p. 38.

[3] 1 Cor. xv. 45.

of the Divine Life, was to bring new vitality to
these timid, nerveless men, fitting them for their
great mission to the world.

In an earlier chapter of his Gospel, S. John
teaches that in the days of our Lord's ministry
*there was as yet no Spirit, because Jesus was not
yet glorified.*[1] The Breath of God could not fall
upon the disciples so long as the Master was
yet in the flesh. Even the Resurrection had not
completed the change which was passing over
Him; He had not yet ascended to the Father,
His body was not yet wholly spiritual; even now,
therefore, the time for the actual descent of the
Spirit had not come. To this extent the ancient
commentator was right who said that 'receive'
in the mouth of the risen Lord meant 'ye shall
receive.'[2] The grant was made at the same time
as the symbolical breathing; they received the
Spirit potentially from that moment, but the actual
outpouring of the Spirit followed the Ascension,
and could not precede it. Nevertheless the Lord's,
'Receive—take—a gift of the Holy Spirit,'[3] was
not an idle form, but a word of power, for it

---

[1] Jo. vii. 39 οὔπω γὰρ ἦν πνεῦμα, ὅτι Ἰησοῦς οὔπω ἐδοξάσθη.

[2] Theodore of Mopsuestia: '*accipite* pro "accipietis" dicit' (Migne, *P.G.* lxvi. 783).

[3] λάβετε πνεῦμα ἅγιον. Compare the anarthrous πνεῦμα in Jo. iii. 5, vii. 39^b, and τὸ πνεῦμα (τὸ ἅγιον) in i. 32, iii. 8, vii. 39^a, xiv. 26.

carried with it the same promise of spiritual life,
to be realized in due time. As the grace of
Ordination and the grace of Confirmation are
gradually fulfilled in the experience of life, so the
original gift of the Spirit bestowed on the Resurrection Day was for the whole life of His Church,
and has manifested itself in every spiritual power
which has worked in the Body of Christ from
the beginning to the present hour. As for the
imperative, it is a warning against a merely passive
attitude on the part of those who receive the
gifts of Christ. As when He gave the Sacrament
of His Body, the Lord said *Take, eat*,[1] so in this
sacramental gift of His Spirit His word again is
'Take'; for this gift, though given absolutely to
the Church, belongs to individual believers only
so far as by an act of the will they severally lay
hold upon it and appropriate it to their own use.

The Church had now been sent and spiritually
equipped for her great task. But what message
was she to deliver? What was the purpose of so
vast a mission, supported by a new inbreathing
into man of a Divine life? The Lord's next words[2]
strike the keynote of the whole movement : *if ye*

---

[1] Mt. λάβετε φάγετε : Mc. simply λάβετε, *take ye* (R.V.).

[2] ἄν τινων ἀφῆτε τὰς ἁμαρτίας, ἀφέωνται· ἄν τινων κρατῆτε, κεκρά-
τηνται. For ἄν (ἐάν) τις cf. Jo. xvi. 23, Acts ix. 2 : in practice it
seems to be nearly equivalent to ὅστις ἄν, but less definite. The
perfects express 'the absolute efficacy of the power' (Westcott).

remit the sins of any, they have been remitted ; if ye retain [the sins] *of any, they have been retained.*[1] This saying is of vital importance for the interpretation of the whole office of the Church.[2]

Shortly after the beginning of His work in Galilee the Lord had pronounced forgiveness to a paralytic who was brought for healing, and had justified His action on the ground that *the Son of Man hath power on earth to forgive sins.*[3] Yet when the Twelve were sent forth into Galilee, though they preached repentance, they received no authority to remit sins ; their powers were limited, so far as we know, to the healing of the sick by unction and the casting out of unclean spirits.[4] To S. Peter, indeed, upon his confession, the Lord had said, *Whatsoever thou shalt bind on earth shall be bound in heaven, and whatsoever thou shalt loose on earth shall be loosed in heaven,*[5] and a similar promise was made to the Church on another occasion.[6] But 'bind' and 'loose' are not synonyms of 'remit' and 'retain'; the former pair of words

---

[1] For κρατεῖν in contrast with ἀφιέναι see Mc. vii. 8. To remit sins is to discharge them, to retain them is to hold them fast, so that the sinner cannot shake them off; see *Report of the Fulham Conference*, 1901-2, p. 5 f.

[2] On its use at Ordinations by the Western Church, see Hooker, *E.P.* v. lxxvii. 5 ff.

[3] Mc. ii. 5, 10.   [4] Mc. vi. 7, 12 f.

[5] Mt. xvi. 19.   [6] Mt. xviii. 18.

describes the entire exercise of the Church's judicial powers, such as the use of discipline, the definition of doctrine, the regulations of Divine worship;[1] the latter is restricted to judgements pronounced *in foro conscientiae*, by the voice of God speaking through the Christian community, or its mouthpiece, the Christian bishops or presbyters. This was a new power, or at least a direction to make a new and far more responsible use of power already given. To remit sins, to retain sins, had been hitherto the exclusive privilege of the Master ; it was henceforth to be exercised in His Name by the members of the Church ; it was to be in fact the *raison d'être* of the Church, the very work which she was sent and inspired to do in the world.

Why was this great commission entrusted to the Church on the evening of the Resurrection Day ? There was much that might have occupied the Lord and His disciples at that first meeting after the Crucifixion ; there were many questions to be asked and answered, many directions to be given. But all these were postponed ; the Lord had weightier business on hand. He had grappled with the great problem of human sin, and had solved it by His sacrifice ; He had come back from the dead with His hands full of gifts for men, first and foremost among which was ' remission

[1] See the *Report* cited above, p. 4.

of sins,' a full discharge from the power of evil for every human being who sought it from Him. But already He was ascending to the Father, and it rested with these men and with those who succeeded them to give effect to the redemption which He had made at so great a cost ; to carry to the world the word of reconciliation, to assure men of their emancipation from sin through the Cross. The hour had struck for committing to the Church this great ministry, and there was not a moment to be lost ; as soon as the disciples knew and believed Him risen, it must be put into their keeping on that very day.

This final revelation of the first Easter Day is the ground of all the healing words and acts of the Christian Church from that day to this. It gives effect to every Sacrament, to every sermon that reaches men's hearts, to the whole service which the Church in her manifold operations renders to sinful humanity ; from the formal absolutions of the ordained priesthood to the simplest words spoken with conviction by the peasant or the child in the Name of Jesus Christ. The whole body of the Church is permeated by the life of the Spirit, in order that in every member, according to the measure of each, it may discharge its Divine work of remitting or, if men will have it so, retaining sins.

We have now finished our brief study of the
manifestations of the risen Lord on the day of
His Resurrection, that great day which determined the future of human nature.[1]   Looking back
upon them, do we not discover traces of an orderly
plan, revealing purpose and progress such as we
might expect to find in the earliest self-manifestations
of the risen Christ?   The Lord was seen first by
Mary of Magdala, the leader of the devoted women
who were 'last at the Cross and earliest at the
grave'; then by Simon Peter, the first of the
Apostles, who of all the Eleven most sorely needed
to be raised from his despair; then to the two on
the way to Emmaus, who belonged to the rank
and file of the unofficial followers; lastly, to the
Eleven and their company, who represented the
whole Christian brotherhood, the Lord's new
'congregation' or Church.[2]   A similar advance may
be marked in the words which were spoken on
these occasions, so far as they are reported.   To
Mary the Lord's message is, *Touch me not . . . I
ascend*—a warning at the outset that the Resurrection is an entrance on a spiritual life, not a return
to the conditions of mortality.   To the disciples
on the way to Emmaus it is an interpretation of

[1] Renan, *Les Apôtres*, p. 23 : 'Tels furent les incidents de ce jour
qui a fixé le sort de l'humanité.'

[2] Mt. xvi. 18, xviii. 17. See Hort, *The Christian Ecclesia*, p. 8 ff.

the Passion in the light of Old Testament history and prophecy—an instruction most needful for men who were finding their way out of Judaism, to whom for the moment the Cross had spelt failure and rejection by God. To the whole brotherhood at the end of that great day the Lord brought the fresh breath of the Spirit, an inspiration which was life from the dead ; and with it a mission which made the Church the messenger of the new life to all mankind.

The appearances on Easter Day, regarded as a whole, bear the stamp of the mind of Jesus Christ ; the Easter sayings are such as no sane criticism can attribute to the imagination of the Apostolic age. It needs a sturdy scepticism to doubt that these narratives rest on a solid basis of fact, or that words so characteristic of the great Master are in substance the words of the risen Christ.

V.

TO THOMAS AND THE REST.

AUTHORITY: Jo. xx. 26-28.

AFTER the Resurrection Day there remained in Jerusalem but one disciple whose sorrow had not been turned into joy.[1] Thomas, though one of the Eleven, was not with them when Jesus came and stood in the midst. He had left the company before Peter returned, certainly before the two had come in from Emmaus. But had he been there to hear their testimony it would have made no difference. When he got back to his brethren, and was met by the joyful tidings, *We have seen the Lord*,[2] he was unconvinced. Nothing would convince him but the evidence of his own senses ; he

---

[1] Jo. xvi. 20.

[2] ἑωράκαμεν τὸν κύριον : cf. v. 18 ἑώρακε τὸν κύριον, v. 29 ἑώρακάς με, and 1 Cor. ix. 1 οὐχὶ Ἰησοῦν τὸν κύριον ἡμῶν ἑώρακα ; The phrase seems to have been current in the Apostolic Church in speaking of a personal experience of the appearances of the risen Christ. The passive form is ὤφθη [ὁ κύριός τινι] ; cf. Lc. xxiv. 24, Acts ix. 17, 1 Cor. xv. 5 ff. Ὤφθη, it should be noted, does not necessarily imply a 'vision'; cf. 3 Regn. xviii. 1 (LXX), Acts vii. 26.

must see for himself, he must handle for himself
the marks of the Crucifixion before he could credit
what they said, that the body which was nailed to
the cross and pierced with a lance had risen from
the tomb. *Except I shall see in his hands the
print of the nails, and put my finger into the print
of the nails, and put my hand into his side, I will
not believe.*

Such an attitude might be caused by widely
different spiritual conditions, and our view of it
must therefore depend upon the estimate which we
form of Thomas's character. Unhappily, little is
really known of the personal history of most of the
Twelve, and Thomas is not an exception, notwithstanding the early apocryphal 'Acts' which profess
to give an account of his life and end. But S. John
has preserved two evidently genuine anecdotes of
this Apostle, which are fairly typical of his attitude
towards life in general and towards Christ. When
the Lord, on receiving the tidings of Lazarus's sick-
ness, proposed to go again into Judaea, where the
Jews had recently sought to stone Him, and the
disciples sought in vain to dissuade Him, it was
Thomas who turned to the rest and said, *Let us
also go, that we may die with him.*[1] The words
shew a desponding spirit, but also an absolute
devotion to the Master, which must be taken into

[1] Jo. xi. 16.

full account in any interpretation of his conduct
after the Resurrection.   Again, when the last evening of the Lord's life had come, and Jesus had said
to the disciples *Whither I go, ye know the way*,[1]
it is Thomas who objects, 'Lord, we know not
whither thou goest; how know we the way?'
Both the frank confession of ignorance and the
bold refusal to accept without explanation the
Master's saying, which seemed to be in conflict with
facts, are characteristic; 'it is almost as though
it were an argument speaking rather than a man.
Yet the argument was no mere sophism; there was
a genuine perplexity within.   The unwillingness to
forego the use of reason even when it weighed in the
balance the Lord's own words was not an impulse
that the Lord could simply rebuke.'[2]   But on that
night after the Resurrection there was no word from
Christ that he himself had heard to be considered,
only the testimony of his fellow-disciples.   It was
simply a question of the value of evidence; was the
evidence of Mary of Magdala, of Peter, of Cleopas
and his friend, even of his ten colleagues and their
whole company, sufficient to override the judgement
which his reason pronounced upon the whole matter?
Certainly it was not; nothing should induce him[3]
to surrender his personal convictions to impressions

[1] Jo. xiv. 4.   [2] Hort, *The Way, the Truth, the Life*, p. 10.
[3] οὐ μὴ πιστεύσω.

produced on the senses of other men.[1]   His devotion
to the Master added strength to his determination,
for it tempted him to believe what he wished to be
true, against the voice of reason ; and such a temptation must be resisted at any cost.   It is not
impossible that with this loyalty to what he supposed to be the course of truth there were mingled
some elements of human weakness : something of
the pride which, having once taken up a position, will
not allow itself to be in the wrong ; the bitterness
of spirit which finds a pleasure in hugging its own
misery ; even the real unbelief which judges it
incredible that God should raise the dead.   The
character of Thomas seems not to have been a
simple one ; there was perhaps in his conduct a
greater mixture of motives than he knew.

The incredulity of Thomas continued through
the week which followed the Resurrection.   But
it did not separate him from the company of his
brother Apostles and disciples.   On the one hand
he was not excluded by the short-sighted
narrowness which sometimes mars the faith of
believers ; on the other, he did not of his own
accord break with his old friends through the
impatience and superciliousness which often attend

[1] There is force in Mr. Latham's remark (p. 79) : 'A person who
is exceptionally clear-sighted within a rather narrow range is apt to
be more impatient than other people when something is put before
him which seems mystical.'

unbelief. He and they were held together by the
power of their common love to the Master—a
love which was as real and deep in Thomas as
in the rest. They believed the Master to be
alive, he regarded Him as dead; a serious difference in a vital matter of faith, yet not so
fundamental as to destroy either devotion to Christ
or communion with His brethren. So it came to
pass that when, on the following Sunday night,
the disciples were again within, Thomas was with
them. Outwardly, everything was as on the evening
of the Resurrection Day. Again the doors were
made fast against the Jews; again, no doubt, the
evening meal was spread, or just ended; again
the company were seated round the great upper
room. Again there appeared in their midst a form
which had not been seen to enter; again there
came from its lips the customary 'Peace,' charged
with no ordinary meaning. But on this occasion
the greeting was followed by no mission to the
world, no insufflation or gift of the Spirit, no
charge to remit or retain sins. These had been
given once for all on Easter night; if Thomas
had not been present and had not believed those
who were, yet he was included in the scope of
the Lord's words, and needed no separate endow-
ment with the powers of the risen Christ. What
he needed was a gift purely personal, the illumi-

nation of faith ; and this the Lord had come to
bestow. It may be asked why, if the message
was for Thomas only and not for the rest, it was
not brought to him when he was alone. Jesus
had sought out Peter, the Apostle who denied
Him, at a time when the other Apostles were not
present ; the restoration to faith of the Apostle
who doubted but remained loyal was effected
before all his brethren.[1]   But the cases differed :
Peter was already penitent, Thomas was still
defiant ; Thomas had rejected the evidence for the
Resurrection in the face of the Church, and in the
face of the Church he must confess his faith.

It is instructive to mark how the Lord con-
quered the doubt of this determined sceptic.   He
gives him precisely the evidence which had been
demanded : *Reach hither thy finger, and see my
hands, and reach hither thy hand and put it into
my side.*   But to say this was really to give far
more than Thomas had asked : there was no need
now to touch the print of the nails or to explore
the pierced side, for the words themselves proved
the identity of Him who spoke them ; who but
the Lord could have overheard the demand which
had been made within closed doors, or have
answered it thus ?   Yet the Lord knew too well
how long the fortress of the will can hold out

[1] See p. 65 f.

when the reason is convinced, and He added a
call to surrender, in which unspeakable tenderness
is mingled with a stern finality: *Be not*—become
not[1]—*faithless, but believing.* Jesus does not account
the scepticism of Thomas thus far as unbelief, but
warns him that it was .on the way to become
so. Thomas stood at the parting of the ways:
the crucial moment of his life had come; he had
reached a supreme test of character. If his doubt
lay deeper than the intellect, if it arose ultimately
from a moral fault, such as pride or self-will,[2] and
he suffered this enemy of God and His Christ to
resist the evidence even when all he had asked
was given and more besides, then indeed his doubt
would grow into unbelief. He must choose, once
for all, between unbelief and faith, and he must
choose at once.

Thomas did not hesitate. His reason convinced,
false pride was thrown aside, and the loyal, loving
heart of the true disciple threw itself at the
Master's feet with an outburst of adoring faith
which leaves S. Peter's great confession far
behind, and even anticipates the convictions of
later Christendom. *Thomas answered and said unto*

[1] μὴ γίνου.

[2] That pride and self-will were mingled with his loyalty to truth,
and threatened to gain the mastery over it, may be freely admitted;
see p. 44. But this had not yet come to pass; he had not 'become
faithless' hitherto.

him,[1] *My Lord and my God*; and Jesus tacitly accepted the tribute as the absolutely sincere homage of a heart that has grasped the innermost truth of His relation to the Father and to men. So it is that doubt, if it is truly 'honest,' *i.e.* if it springs from nothing but the fear of exceeding known truth and sinning against the light of reason, may be the forerunner of the fullest, most convinced, belief, a belief greatly stronger and more deeply rooted than any which comes of the easy acceptance of a traditional creed.

The conversion of Thomas was complete ; his faith rose to a maturity of which the Gospels supply no other example. Yet the Lord did not congratulate Thomas as He had congratulated Simon Peter.[2] He did not answer, 'Blessed art thou, Thomas, because thou hast believed'; but only, *Hast thou believed because thou hast seen ?* [3] *blessed are they who saw not, and believed.'* [4]   His congratulation is reserved for those who come to faith by another road than that of sight. The Lord, in His Divine-human consciousness, projects Himself into the coming centuries, and sees not only

---

[1] As Bp. Westcott points out 'the words are beyond question addressed to Christ (*saith unto him*) and cannot but be understood as a confession of belief as to His Person.'

[2] Mt. xvi. 17.   [3] Or, *Thou hast believed*, etc.

[4] μακάριοι οἱ μὴ ἰδόντες καὶ πιστεύσαντες.

the thousands who will believe Him risen on the testimony of the first eye-witnesses, but the millions who, when the eye-witnesses are gone, will trust the written page of the Gospels, or the spoken word of His messengers. Their lot will, in a manner, be more enviable than that of the Eleven in those happy hours after the Resurrection, because it will imply a higher faith, resting on the experience of life and the possession of the Spirit of the risen Christ. *Belief*, under ordinary and normal conditions, *cometh of hearing*,[1] not of seeing. Even before the end of the Apostolic age the Lord's words proved themselves true, and S. Peter, who himself had believed because he had seen, was able to speak to the Churches of Asia Minor of One *whom not having seen ye love ; in whom, though now ye see him not, yet believing, ye rejoice greatly with joy unspeakable and glorified.*[2] The joy of the first Easter is more than fulfilled, as the season comes round year by year, in the joy of the living Church which believes on a risen Christ whom, as yet, it has not seen.

After the appearance to Thomas we hear no more of the Lord's body being offered to the

[1] Rom. x. 17 ἡ πίστις ἐξ ἀκοῆς.

[2] 1 Pet. i. 8 οὐκ ἰδόντες . . . μὴ ὁρῶντες—'the first is a direct statement of historical fact, the second is introduced as it were hypothetically' (Hort).

touch of any of His disciples. The prohibition, *Touch me not*, was removed, and even reversed in the case of the Eleven, who were to be the witnesses of the Resurrection to the world;[1] to these the Lord not only shewed Himself alive, but He submitted His body to their scrutiny, and even ate and drank in their presence. It was an exception to a rule, which we can see to have been necessary in the circumstances. But it creates in many minds a difficulty which, in our present ignorance, cannot be wholly removed. How such properties as to be tangible, to bear the imprints of nails or a spear wound, to be able to partake of food, can be reconciled with the power of becoming invisible at will, or with any conception which can be formed of a spiritual body, we do not know. But the limitations of our knowledge ought to be no hindrance to belief, if we bear in mind that the Resurrection of Jesus Christ is, *ex hypothesi*, a fact unique in human experience, and that the border-land of flesh and spirit, to which the risen body of the Lord seems to have belonged during the forty days, is an unexplored territory of which no man can speak with confidence on this side of the grave.

[1] Acts x. 40 ff.

VI.

TO THE SEVEN, BY THE LAKE.

AUTHORITIES: Jo. xxi. 1-23; Gospel of Peter (?) 12.

WE have now reached a difficulty which has given some occasion ·to those who are disposed to doubt the truth of the Resurrection narratives, and some uneasiness to those who believe.

The Marcan tradition[1] represents the angel at the tomb as saying to the women on the morning of the Resurrection Day, *Go tell his disciples and Peter, He goeth before you into Galilee; there shall ye see him*; and the first Gospel adds that this message was endorsed by the risen Lord Himself, in whose mouth it became an explicit direction to the Eleven to return to the north : *Go tell my brethren that they depart into Galilee.* S. Luke, however, shews no knowledge of any such precept, or of any return from Jerusalem ; while S. John, who places one of the appearances in Galilee, keeps the Eleven in Jerusalem for a full week after Easter Day.

[1] Mc., Mt.

If the Apostles received from the women the
message of the angel, it is strange that they should
have lingered in Jerusalem after their business
was done.[1] It is true that the seven days of the
feast were not ended before Thursday night on
the week following the Resurrection, and as the
Gospel of Peter suggests, it may have been
expedient to remain till then, in order to return
in the caravan with other Galilean visitors.[2] But
why should they have stayed to the octave of the
Resurrection? Had the Lord Himself at His first
meeting with the Eleven arranged another meeting
on the evening of the first day of the following
week? Was it His purpose in this way to suggest
a weekly commemoration of the Resurrection, at
which, after the Ascension, His Church might
still meet with Him in the breaking of the
Bread?[3] Who that realizes the foresight and
forethought of the Master can doubt that this
is a possible explanation of the prolonged stay in
the city? If so, the problem is partly solved.

[1] Renan (*Les Apôtres*, p. 28) speaks of the *nostalgie* which forced
them to return. There is certainly no trace of home-sickness in
their conduct, as the Gospels describe it.

[2] Petr. ev. 12 ἦν δὲ τελευταία ἡμέρα τῶν ἀζύμων καὶ πολλοί
τινες ἐξήρχοντο, ὑποστρέφοντες εἰς τοὺς οἴκους αὐτῶν τῆς ἑορτῆς
παυσαμένης.

[3] Latham (p. 175) thinks that His intention was to provide a time
of rest and quiet for the quickening of the 'seed thoughts' sown
upon Easter Day.

There remains, however, the apparent inconsistency between the statement that the Lord was going into Galilee, followed by the words, *There shall ye see him*, and the facts for which the third and fourth Gospels vouch, that He appeared to the Eleven in Jerusalem, and that whether by His command or not, they remained in the city for at least a week after the Resurrection. But again the difficulty may be due to imperfect knowledge. We possess but fragments of the story, and we must not wonder if we cannot always piece them together. What if the promise that the Eleven should see the risen Lord in Galilee referred only to the greater manifestations, the larger visions, which were to be vouchsafed among the scenes of the ministry? As for S. Luke's complete silence as to a return to the north, it is unreasonable to construe it as an argument against the Marcan tradition. There is reason to think that the third Evangelist had before him the work of the second, and if he omitted all reference to the Galilean appearances, he did so because he had access to other information which would fully occupy his space. He tells the Emmaus incident at such length that he finds it necessary to pass on from the Resurrection to the Ascension without giving more than a bare summary of the teaching of the intermediate days ; for he is hurry-

ing on to a second part of his history which
will begin with another short account of the same
period, so far as it may be necessary to intro-
duce the story of the Ascension and the post-
Ascension work of the Church.[1]

The order of the appearances in Galilee cannot
be determined with certainty. But it will be
convenient to begin with the incident which the
appendix to S. John [2] places next after the appearances to Thomas and the Ten, and regards as third
among the greater manifestations of the forty days.[3]

The Gospel of Peter, after relating the return
of the Galilean visitors, proceeds; 'But I, Simon
Peter, and Andrew my brother, took our nets and
went to the sea, and there was with us Levi,
the son of Alphaeus, whom the Lord' . . . Here
the fragment ends abruptly. But it can scarcely
be doubted that the writer is about to relate the
incident which we find in the appendix to S.
John. The group indeed is not quite the same;

[1] Acts i. 1-11. It is true that even here S. Luke does not mention
Galilee. But (1) Jerusalem is the centre of interest in view of the
history of the Acts, and (2) in so brief a summary he has no
occasion to enter into details as to the locality of the appearances.

[2] Jo. xxi. stands on a different plane from Mc. xvi. 9-20, being
clearly the work of the writer or school of writers to whom we
owe the rest of the Gospel: cf. Sanday, *Criticism of the Fourth
Gospel*, pp. 63, 80 f.

[3] Jo. xxi. 14. Not absolutely the third, since according to *c*. xx.
the Lord had appeared at least three times before.

in the Petrine Gospel it consists of Peter, Andrew,
and Matthew; in the Johannine Gospel, of Peter,
Thomas, Nathanael, the sons of Zebedee, and two
unnamed disciples, who may have been Andrew
and Matthew, though the suppression of their
names is against this identification. But in one
important point the two accounts agree; both
represent the disciples as going back to their
occupation on the Lake. 'We took our nets,'[1]
Peter is made to say by the Petrine writer; *I
go a-fishing*, he says in S. John's story, whereupon
the rest answer, *We also come with thee.* One
asks oneself with what purpose Peter and his
party returned to their nets: whether it was
merely to provide themselves with a meal, or
whether with the intention of resuming their old
life. Had they forgotten the great work opened
before them by the commission received on Easter
night? or had they never realized its meaning?
No doubt it was a time of waiting, of uncertainty,
even of suspense; nearly a fortnight had passed
since the Resurrection, and no plans had yet
been formed for the future.[2] It may have been
that a crisis was near; a little further delay, and
Peter and the rest might have once more become

[1] τὰ λίνα ; so cod. 604=700 at Mc. i. 18.

[2] That a great future was before them was implied by the words
in Jo. xx. 21 ff. ; but no details had been given.

mere fishermen. But this danger had not been overlooked ; the Good Shepherd had gone before His sheep and interposed His guidance at the moment when it was needed.

The fishing that night was a failure; they caught nothing. Simon Peter may have recalled a fruitless night spent upon the Lake two or three years ago, and how on that occasion the Master had filled their nets. Would that He were in the boat with them now, to bid them let down the nets and find! As the morning began to break, a solitary figure was seen standing on the shell-strewn shore.[1] The man, whoever he was, hailed them : *Children, have you any fish for your meal?*[2] Through the clear morning air there came across the water the answer *No*. The stranger replied, *Cast the net to the right of the boat, and you shall find*. They may have thought that from his place on the shore he could see a shoal of fish that lay in the shallows to their right, but had escaped the notice of those who were in the boat. So the net was thrown as he directed, and at once it was heavy with fish—too heavy to be drawn up again into the boat. All that could be done was to bring the boat to shore, dragging

[1] εἰς τὸν αἰγιαλόν.

[2] μή τι προσφάγιον ἔχετε, *i.e.* 'any relish to eat with your bread.' Μή τι, as Westcott observes, anticipates the negative answer that follows ; the Lord knew how matters stood with them.

the net after it; and when it was close to land, to draw the net up on the beach. It was then found that the net had not been broken by the weight,[1] though the fishes, which were now rapidly sorted by the fishermen,[2] were of great size, and numbered, as John well remembered, one hundred and fifty-three—a record haul indeed.

Meanwhile the Lord had been recognized. The discovery was made while the boat was still some distance from the land by 'the disciple whom Jesus loved,' who, if not John the son of Zebedee, must have been one of the two unnamed disciples in the boat. His special devotion to the Master, which answered to the Master's special love for him, made him quicker than the rest to realize that 'it was the Lord.'[3] But he was not the first to act upon his own discovery. As at the tomb on Easter day it was John who was the first to arrive, but Peter who first entered,[4] so ˌnow Peter, though behind John in reaching the truth, was before him in action. In an instant he had clad himself in his fisherman's blouse—for he had been stripped for work—girded it round him,[5]

---

[1] Contrast Lc. v. 6 διερήσσετο δὲ τὰ δίκτυα αὐτῶν.

[2] Cf. Mt. xiii. 48, where the familiar scene is depicted.

[3] ὁ κύριός ἐστιν.   [4] Jo. xx. 4 ff.

[5] τὸν ἐπενδύτην διεζώσατο. Cf. v. 18 ἐζώννυες σεαυτόν, and 1 Pet. v. 3 τὴν ταπεινοφροσύνην ἐγκομβώσασθε—a reminiscence perhaps of the rough fisherman's dress.

plunged into the sea, and was already swimming or wading to the shore. No one should be before him in greeting the Master on His return to Galilee.

As the boat approached the shore, it was seen that a charcoal fire [1] was burning on the beach, with fish and bread laid upon it. We are reminded of Elijah who, on awakening from his sleep in the wilderness, found a cake baken on the coals ready for his refreshment.[2] But the Lord did not provide for the wants of the whole party : there was more than enough at hand of their own taking. *Bring of the fish which ye have now caught* is His next word ; and when that has been done, *Come and break your fast.* The commands, trivial as they seem on the lips of One who has recently conquered Death, are characteristic of Him who in His mortal life had ever shewn Himself mindful of the needs of mortal men,[3] and yet had never supplied by miracle what could be provided by ordinary means.

The meal proceeded in silence. Jesus Himself passed from one to another, bringing to each the bread and fish. No one dared ask [4] who He was,

---

[1] ἀνθρακίαν.   [2] 1 Kings xix. 6.

[3] Latham, p. 258: 'He will lay no strain of emotion on hungry and wearied men.'

[4] ἐξετάσαι αὐτὸν 'question Him.' The question would imply some lurking doubt, and doubt, they felt, there was really none. 'A

for all by this time knew Him to be the Lord.
Yet though He came close to each of them, the
recognition seems to have been brought about by
what He said and did rather than by His bodily
appearance. Some kind of change perhaps had
passed over the features ; the beginning of the
final change which transforms the natural body into
the spiritual. The image of the heavenly was
already upon Him, so that those who had been
with Him so long in Galilee would not have known
Him by His face alone.[1]

When breakfast was ended, the purpose of this
fresh manifestation began to reveal itself. Suddenly
the Lord turned to Peter and asked, *Simon, son
of John,*[2] *lovest thou me more than these?* ' *Simon,
son of John,*' recalls *Simon Barjonah,* which, on the
great day of Simon's confession, the Master had
changed to Simon Peter.[3] Now He purposely
reverts to the patronymic of Simon's early life, and
addresses him as the natural man, not as the
spiritual. His fall had forfeited the name which
his faith had won, and put him back into the days
of mere discipleship ; he must prove his right
to the title of the ' Rock ' by a new and greater

graphic picture of the hushed wonder and awe with which the
Apostles beheld what had passed' (Sanday, *Authorship of the
Fourth Gospel,* p. 268).

[1] See p. 21 ff.   [2] Ἰωάνου, cf. Jo. i. 42 ; the Greek equivalent of Ἰωνᾶς.
[3] Mt. xvi. 17 f.

confession—a confession not of faith, but of love.
'Lovest thou me more than these, the rest of my
disciples, love me?' Simon had claimed to do so
before he fell: *though all men shall be offended*,
he had said, *yet will not I*;[1] could he now sub-
stantiate this claim? would he even dare to repeat
it? Three times the question is asked, for Simon
had three times denied the Lord; but the second
and third times the words 'more than these' are
dropped, for that part of the challenge is not taken
up. On the other hand, Simon does not hesitate
to profess his love for Jesus, and to repeat the
profession as often as the Master asks for it,
substituting only, as S. John remembered, or as he
interpreted the answers, a word less far reaching
than that which was used in the questions, as if
he were no longer sure that his love rose to the
height of a spiritual, supernatural grace.[2] The
Lord, who knows all things, knows that he, Simon,
son of John, is at least loyal and true in the
depths of his true self. He may not love with
the spiritual fervour of the beloved disciple: he
may not love more truly, more fervently than any
other of the disciples; but his devotion, such as
it is, is sincere; of that He is sure, and the

[1] Mt. xxvi. 33.

[2] The Lord asks ἀγαπᾷς; Simon answers φιλῶ. In the third question
this change is accepted, and φιλεῖς takes the place of ἀγαπᾷς.

Searcher of hearts[1] can testify from His own observation that it is so.

But Jesus does not answer, as Simon perhaps expected, 'Yea, I know that thou lovest me.' Each protestation of love is simply followed by a demand for proof of its reality and permanence. *Feed my lambs : tend my sheep : feed my sheep.*[2] The three charges are progressive, and include the whole duty of the pastoral office : a duty which extends both to the young and immature, and to the older and riper members of the flock ; which embraces both the feeding of all with food convenient for them, and the guidance and government of the entire Church. So the Chief Shepherd of the sheep[3] commits to the care of the disciple who professed to love Him the pastoral work, which by his fall he had forfeited. Simon is readmitted to this apostolate, and at the same time provided with a vast field of labour in which he must demonstrate his love till his life's end. For the sheep are not Peter's, but Christ's, and he must feed them because

---

[1] σὺ οἶδας . . . σὺ οἶδας . . . πάντα σὺ οἶδας· σὺ γινώσκεις. Cf. Jo. ii. 23 διὰ τὸ αὐτὸν γινώσκειν πάντας καὶ ὅτι οὐ χρείαν εἶχεν ἵνα τις μαρτυρήσῃ περὶ τοῦ ἀνθρώπου.

[2] βόσκε . . . ποίμαινε . . . βόσκε. Simon the fisherman must henceforth become Simon the shepherd ; cf. 1 Peter v. 2, and contrast Lc. v. 10.

[3] 1 Pet. v. 4 ὁ ἀρχιποίμην. Just before we have ποιμάνατε τὸ ἐν ὑμῖν ποίμνιον τοῦ θεοῦ. The whole passage seems to be a reminiscence of the present scene ; see p. 57, note 5.

they are Christ's and for Christ's sake, because he
loves Christ.[1]   What the end will be, he is warned ;
it will be no visible reward for his work, but on
the contrary, a final and severest test of the sincerity
of his devotion. *Verily, verily, I say unto thee,
When thou wast young, thou girdedst thyself, and
walkedst whither thou wouldest ; but when thou shalt
be old, thou shalt stretch forth thy hands and another
shall gird thee, and carry thee whither thou wouldest
not.*   To Simon, naturally impulsive and independent, accustomed, too, from his youth to the free
life of the Galilean fisherman, which he had just
begun to taste again, the very thought of anything
like restraint or compulsion was odious ; yet this
also he must ultimately undergo for the Master's
sake.   When he had grown old in the exacting
pastoral work now laid upon him, his life of
unremitting service must be crowned by a violent
death ; his impetuous, fiery spirit would be called
to submit itself to the rough handling of the jailor
and the executioner.   The scene itself is mercifully
veiled in enigmatic words,[2] but the writer of the

---

[1] Augustine: 'si me diligis, non te pascere cogita, sed oves meas ; sicut
meas pasce non sicut tuas ; gloriam meam in eis quaere, non tuam.'

[2] ἐκτενεῖς τὰς χεῖράς σου καὶ ἄλλος ζώσει σε does not clearly indicate
crucifixion or anything more than captivity.   As Dr. Sanday has
pointed out (*Authorship of S. John's Gospel*, p. 269), 'the prophecy is
attested as historical by its vagueness' ; moreover, 'it speaks well for
the conscientiousness of the Evangelist that he has not accommodated
his description more closely to the circumstances.'

fourth Gospel, who survived S. Peter by forty
years, on looking back saw in them a picture of
the death by which that Apostle was called in his
old age to *glorify God*. Simon Peter, as we learn
from Tertullian,[1] was crucified under Nero ; and we
know also that when the time came, though his
flesh doubtless shrank, as the flesh of the Lord
Himself had shrunk, from the cross, his spirit
embraced it for the Master's sake.[2] So both his
faith and his love were finally approved. But all
this was as yet in the womb of time ; meanwhile
there was one duty which called him to immediate
action. *When he had spoken thus he saith unto
him, Follow me.* Once again, as in the first days
of the Galilean ministry, there came the call which
strikes the keynote of the whole Christian life.
Peter had fallen, and must begin again, although
in a new way and with larger aims.

It is characteristic of S. Peter that his thoughts
should rebound by a quick transition from his own
future to that of his colleagues ; it was a relief to
escape from the strain of intensely personal considera-
tions, to divert attention from himself to another.[3]

---

[1] Tert. *Scorp.* 14 : 'tunc Petrus ab altero cingitur, cum cruci adstringitur.'

[2] Orig. ap. Eus. *H. E.* iii. 1 : ἐπὶ τέλει ἐν Ῥώμῃ γενόμενος ἀνεσκολο-
πίσθη κατὰ κεφαλῆς, οὕτως αὐτὸς ἀξιώσας παθεῖν.

[3] Curiosity was another personal feature ; cf. Latham, p. 265, who
compares the incident in Jo. xiii. 24. Is S. Peter thinking of his
own early fault when he warns Christians against being ἀλλοτριο-
επίσκοποι ? (1 Pet. iv. 15).

The party had left the place where they had breakfasted, the Lord going first and Peter following, when Peter, turning round, saw John behind him. If he, Simon, were destined to such a life of constant service, to so bitter an end, what was in store for the disciple whom Jesus loved? There could be no doubt of John's love for Jesus, of its reality, or of its spiritual elevation; but how was it to be manifested to the world? Was he also to receive some great pastoral charge? Was he also, at the end of a long life of service, to suffer for the Master's sake? His impatience to know broke out into a rash question, of which the very form seems to have been preserved: *Lord, what of this man?*[1] what is he to do? But Peter gained nothing by his curiosity but a rebuke, and a renewal of the personal command: *If I will that he tarry while I am coming,*[2] *what is that to thee? follow thou me.*[3] Strange that the restoration of this great Apostle should need to be balanced, like the reward of his confession, by a stern reproof! He was still unable, as it appears, to bear anything which made him conspicuous; it brought self-importance, and as a

---

[1] οὗτος δὲ τί;

[2] ἕως ἔρχομαι: cf. Lc. xix. 13 ἐν ᾧ ἔρχομαι.

[3] 'Thou' is emphatic (σύ μοι ἀκολούθει); 'as for thee, follow me—that is all.'

consequence, unseemly conduct.   And it belongs
to the Divine love of the Master not to spare
reproof when it is needed, even as on the other
hand He does not fail to recognize faith or love
or repentance when any of these meets His eye.

The words in which the Lord rebuked Simon's
curiosity threw no light on the future of S. John.
They were understood, indeed, to mean that John
should survive to the Parousia, and be among
those who should not die but be changed at the
Coming of the Lord.   Possibly John himself had
so understood them ; but as the years went on,
and it became apparent that the hope of an
imminent Return must be abandoned, he saw
that the Lord had in fact made no such promise,
but merely asserted His purpose to deal with each
disciple according to His will.   It was no concern
of Peter to know how He would deal with another
of His servants ; if John were called to live to
the end of the age, that would not touch the
question of Peter's career or of his duty.

It may be asked in what relation this interview
stands with that which was vouchsafed to Simon
on the Resurrection Day.   On both occasions, it
may be supposed, the Lord dealt with the situation
created by Peter's fall.   That event affected Peter
on two sides of his life : as a disciple, and as
an Apostle.   In the private interview on Easter

E

day relief had been bought, we may well believe, to his personal grief; he had been assured of the Lord's forgiveness, and his wound was healed. But there remained the question whether he had not forfeited by his sin the Apostolic office; whether one who had denied his Lord could be used by Him in the work of building the Church. To this doubt, present in the mind of Peter, if not in the minds of the rest, the Lord gave a public answer; for the matter was one which it concerned not Peter only, but the whole Church to know.   Peter had thrice denied, and thrice the pastoral office was again committed to his hands. Perhaps, indeed, no member of the Apostolic College was so well qualified to feed the flock of God as one who had himself known the bitterness of breaking loose from the fold, and who had been sought and brought back to it by the love of the Supreme Pastor and Bishop of souls.

VII.

TO THE ELEVEN, ON THE HILLS.

AUTHORITIES: Mt. xxviii. 16-20; 'Mc.' xvi. 15-18; 1 Cor. xv. 6.

WE have now lost the guidance of S. John, but S. Matthew[1] at this point takes his place, and leads us on to a second great manifestation which took place in Galilee. On this occasion the Lord met the Eleven at a place previously determined;[2] they *went into Galilee,* unto *the mountain where Jesus had appointed them.*[3] The appointment might have been made before they left Jerusalem, as the context in S. Matthew seems to suggest; or at the meeting with the seven disciples by the shore of the lake. In either case the 'mountain' which was intended is probably the high ground above the lake[4] rather than an isolated hill. The informal

---

[1] xxviii. 16 ff.

[2] A unique instance, unless the meeting on the first Sunday after Easter was prearranged; see p. 52.

[3] οὗ ἐτάξατο αὐτοῖς ὁ Ἰησοῦς.

[4] So τὸ ὄρος is used in Mt. xiv. 23, xv. 29, and probably also in v. 1, viii. 1. Contrast ὄρος ὑψηλόν (xvii. 1), where a particular summit is in view. Ἡ ὀρεινή is used only in Lc. i. 39, 65.

gathering by the seashore was to be followed by
a solemn interview with the Eleven on the heights
where they had received their appointment to the
apostolic office.[1]

It may be assumed that the day was fixed as
well as the place of meeting. We can imagine
the eagerness with which the Eleven went up into
the hills. They would remind themselves how in
the early days of the ministry they had sought
Jesus in a desert place,[2] and now they were seeking
Him again, but in circumstances how different !
As they ascend, an eager outlook is kept. At
length the form of a man is seen coming towards
them, but still at some distance—on the further
side of a wady, it may have been, or just on the
ridge of an opposite hill. Those who first saw
Him at once exclaimed ' It is the Lord !' and the
greater part when they heard it fell upon their
faces,[3] to do homage to the risen Christ. Some,
however, there were who held back, hesitating[4] as
men who were of two minds, hoping, half believing
that it was the Lord, but unwilling to commit
themselves until they saw Him near at hand, and
knew that it was indeed the Master. Too much has

---

[1] Mc. iii. 13.   [2] Mc. i. 36.

[3] προσεκύνησαν, not simply ἐγονυπέτησαν. Once during the ministry
the Twelve had prostrated themselves, but at a moment of unusual
awe (Mt. xiv. 33). Cf. Lc. xxiv. 52.

[4] ἐδίστασαν.

been made of this hesitation, as if it implied that even after the appearances of Easter night and the Sunday after Easter there were still among the Apostles themselves those who doubted of the fact of the Resurrection. It is by no means certain that the Eleven were alone on this occasion,[1] and if they were not, the doubt may have been limited to those in their company. But at a distance even the Eleven may not have been all equally convinced of the identity of the person whom they saw at a distance with the Lord. In any case it was not the fact of the Resurrection that they doubted, but merely whether this was the risen Christ.

All doubt vanished when Jesus approached[2] and spoke to them. The words were spoken in the tone of ordinary conversation, with which they were familiar; but never had human lips, even the lips of the Son of Man, spoken thus before. *All authority was given to me in heaven and upon earth. Go therefore and disciple all the nations, baptizing them into the name of the Father and the Son and the Holy Spirit; teaching them to keep all things whatsoever I enjoined upon you*

[1] See p. 82 f.

[2] προσελθὼν . . . ἐλάλησεν αὐτοῖς. For προσέρχεσθαι in this sense see Mt. xvii. 7; for λαλεῖν, of the half-colloquial mode of discourse adopted by our Lord, Mt. xii. 46, xiii. 3.

And behold, I am with you all the days until the consummation of the age.

The Lord begins with a characteristic claim of 'authority.'[1] As He gave authority to His disciples to act in His name,[2] so He spoke of Himself as One who had received authority from the Father.[3] The field of His own authority seems to grow as His ministry advances; at the outset He has authority to forgive sins on earth; as the days pass on, we read of authority to act as the final judge of all human lives, to determine the bounds of His own life, laying it down and taking it up at pleasure; on the eve of the Passion He speaks of authority given to Him over all flesh, *i.e.* all mankind.[3] But none of these great claims reaches the boundless magnificence of the words, *All authority was given to me in heaven and on earth.* They are words which fairly take our breath away, if we realize that they were spoken on the earth by man to men. It is not so much the claim to 'all authority on earth' that staggers us, for there is a sense in which a great religious teacher may exercise universal power over mankind; and throughout the greater part of the civilized world

[1] ἐξουσία, not δύναμις, right rather than might, though He possessed that also. But He emphasizes, as always, the authority which lay at the root of His displays of power.

[2] Mt. x. 1, Lc. x. 19, xix. 17.

[3] Mc. ii. 10, Jo. v. 27, x. 18, xvii. 2.

our Lord is in this sense actually ' Lord of lords
and King of kings.' The Cross already stands
above the Crown. But authority 'in heaven,' in
that unseen and eternal order which is altogether
beyond human knowledge or control, is another
matter; yet this also is claimed by the risen
Christ. It is the unique reward of His unique
victory over sin and death that all spiritual powers,
no less than those which move the phenomenal
world, are put under His feet. At the beginning
of His ministry the Tempter had shewn Him all
the kingdoms of the world and the glory of them,
and promised to give Him all if He would do
homage to Evil.[1] And now, at the end of His
career, He has gained all these and infinitely more
by His refusal. The Father, whom He obeyed
even unto death, has set Him *far above all rule
and authority and power and dominion, and every
name that is named, not only in this world, but also
in that which is to come.*[2]

But what is the purpose for which the Lord
speaks on this occasion of His immense authority?
The next words explain: *Go ye therefore and
disciple all the nations.* The Eleven are to be
sent on an oecumenical mission, and they must
know that they have behind them an authority

[1] Mt. iv. 9. Cf. H. J. C. Knight, *The Temptation*, p. 112 ff.
[2] Eph. i. 21 ; cf. Phil. ii. 9 ff., Col. i. 16, 20, ii. 10.

which is oecumenical. Their mission, although
fulfilled on earth, will deal with things belonging
to the unseen order, and they must know that they
have been sent by One who has authority in heaven
as well as on earth. For both needs the Lord's
great saying provides.

On Easter night the Lord had already entrusted
them with a mission to which were attached spiritual
powers : *As my Father hath sent me, even so send
I you . . . receive ye the Holy Ghost.* But whither
was He sending them ? When they were sent into
the towns and villages of Galilee their commission
ran, *Go not into any way of the Gentiles, and enter
not into any city of the Samaritans ; but go
rather to the lost sheep of the house of Israel.*[1] But
now this restriction is not only taken off, but the
original precept is almost reversed ; they are sent
not to Israel, but to all the nations, the heathen
nations, of the world.[2] The contrast between the
two commands is as great as possible ; and the post-
Resurrection charge is 'thrown into brilliant relief.'
Yet there is no inconsistency. The barriers imposed
by the Lord at the first sending of the Twelve were
temporary ; the full tide of spiritual life which came

[1] Mt. x. 5.

[2] πάντα τὰ ἔθνη, not perhaps excluding the λαός, but certainly
emphasizing the Gentile world as the chief scene of the Church's
future work. Contrast Lc. ii. 32.

in with the Resurrection has swept them away;
universal authority is now in the hands of Jesus
Christ, and with it has come the universal mission
of His Church. The Eleven, it need scarcely be
said, must have failed to grasp the full meaning
of their new commission at the time when it was
given. Then and for years afterwards a mission to
the Gentiles could only mean to them a mission
to bring the nations into the fold of Judaism by
preaching the faith of Jesus the Messiah. It may
be doubted whether the original Apostolate, with
a few exceptions, ever fully understood either the
words of Christ on the Galilean hills or even such
events as the vision of S. Peter and the call and
preaching of S. Paul. Nevertheless, the greatest
saying of the risen Lord bore fruit in due
season. From the first it outlined the policy
of the future Church, and it has inspired all her
missionary work from the first century to the
twentieth. To-day, in the yearly increasing facili-
ties of intercourse between the peoples of the
world, we hear afresh the call, *Go, disciple*[1] *all
the nations.*

The Lord adds his directions how this is to be
done. First by baptizing them. John the Forerunner had made disciples in this way, and the early

[1] $\mu\alpha\theta\eta\tau\epsilon\acute{\nu}\sigma\alpha\tau\epsilon$: a Matthaean word (xiii. 52, xxvii. 57, xxviii. 19),
but occurring also once in the Acts (xiv. 21).

disciples of Jesus had followed his example,[1] but apparently only for a short time, and in Judaea : in Galilee a disciple of Jesus seems to have been known only by his personal attendance on the Master. Such attendance was now impracticable, for the Lord was withdrawing Himself from the visible world. The great oecumenical society, the Catholic Church which was to embrace all nations, needed some note of discipleship which was universally applicable, and Baptism was such a note, and was already familiar to the Eleven in this light. So Baptism was revived, and made the first sacrament of the new order. But Jesus never simply continues the old ; in the very act of reviving it, He invests it with new powers, the powers of the world to come. His Baptism is to be not simply a Baptism of repentance, but a Baptism *into the name of the Father and the Son and the Holy Spirit*.[2]

These last words have commonly been regarded as a form prescribed by Christ for use in the act of baptizing, and they have been used in this

---

[1] Jo. iv. 1.

[2] Because Eusebius of Caesarea in quoting Mt. xxviii. 19 often omits or varies these words, it has been recently conjectured that they were an early interpolation into the saying of Christ. But the conjecture has no support from MSS. or versions of the N.T. or from other patristic writers. The whole question is discussed by Bp. Chase in the *Journal of Theological Studies*, vi. p. 131 ff.

way by the Church from the second century.[1]   But
there is no evidence that they were so understood
from the first; certainly there is no reference to
them in any of the references to the administration of Christian Baptism which are found in the
Acts and Epistles.   Men are said to have been
baptized *into the name of Lord Jesus*,[2] or *into
Christ*,[3] and not into the Name of the Three.   Well
advised as the Church has doubtless been in adopt-
ing the very words of Christ as the formula of
Christian Baptism, it is probable that they were
spoken with the more important purpose of invest-
ing Baptism with a significance which did not
belong to earlier rites.   The essence of Christian
Baptism, according to this saying, is that it introduces men into a mystical relation to the Father,
the Son, and the Holy Spirit, and marks them as
consecrated to the service of the Three,[4] as being
in some high sense identified with the Three to
whom henceforth he belongs.   This is to us a

[1] See *Didache*, 7; Justin, *Apol.* i. 61; Tertullian, *de baptismo*, 6.

[2] Acts. ii. 38, viii. 16, x. 48, xix. 5.

[3] Rom. vi. 3, Gal. iii. 27.

[4] In such a phrase the name is not the mere title by which a
person is known, but rather the person himself, so that baptism
into the name of the Three is a dedication to Their use and owner-
ship.   See Deissmann (*Bible Studies*, p. 146 f., 197 ff.), who quotes
from the papyri the phrase ἔντευξις εἰς τὸ ὄνομα τοῦ βασιλέως, a
petition to the king's majesty.

familiar conception, but to the Eleven, so far as
they understood it, it was the crowning revelation
of the Lord's teaching. Not only did it give to
the rite of Baptism a meaning which was then
entirely new, and which transformed a ceremonial
purification into *the washing of regeneration and
renewing of the Holy Ghost*,[1] but it gathered up
into a single sentence the whole theology of the
ministry, and thus laid the basis of the Christian
creed as well as of the Christian life. In the Lord's
earlier sayings we hear much of the Father; much
also, in the fourth Gospel at least, of the Son;[2]
something again, but this also chiefly in S. John,
of the Holy Spirit; but the Three are not named
in the same breath, or in close association, except in
the last discourse, where it is said that the Father
will send the Spirit in the name of Jesus Christ,
or that Jesus Christ will send the Spirit from the
Father[3]; and there it is matter of inference rather
than of direct teaching, that the Father, the Son, and
the Holy Spirit are related in any such manner, that
they could be represented as claiming equally and
together the whole service of man. It is certainly
surprising to find in the first Gospel such an
anticipation of the later doctrine of the Holy
Trinity; we should have expected it, if anywhere,

[1] Tit. iii. 5.   [2] Cf. however Mt. xi. 27, xxiv. 36.
[3] Jo. xiv. 16 f., 26; xv. 26.

in the fourth. There are, therefore, scholars of undoubted orthodoxy, who suggest that in reporting this saying of the risen Christ S. Matthew has perhaps unconsciously substituted the familiar phraseology of his own generation for the actual words of the Lord.[1] But what reason is there to suppose that the phraseology was familiar at the time when the editor of the first Gospel wrote? Certainly the actual form of words is not found elsewhere in the New Testament, or in other Christian writings of the first century.[2] On the other hand, there are trinitarian passages in the earliest Christian literature which are not easily to be explained, unless we may suppose that the Lord Himself had associated the Father, the Son, and the Spirit in some saying attributed to Him by the tradition of the first generation.[3] Nor can it be held that the saying in Matt. xxviii. 19, is either beyond the competence of the risen Christ to utter, or inconsistent with any of His earlier sayings; on the contrary, it forms a magnificent summary of all His scattered teaching about the Father, the Spirit, and His own relations to

[1] The Dean of Westminster seems to incline to this view in *Encyclop. Bibl.* art. 'Baptism'; and see W. C. Allen, *S. Matthew*, p. 307.

[2] The nearest approach to it, in the received text of 1 Jo. v. 7, is now acknowledged on all hands to be an interpolation.

[3] *e.g.* 2 Cor. xiii. 14; Eph. iv. 4, 5; 1 Pet. i. 2; Rev. i. 4, 5; Clem. R. *Cor.* 46. 6.

both. The Lord does not, indeed, in this summary, deliver a dogma to be preached; He communicates a life rather than a creed—a life of fellowship, of consecration, of Divine fulness and strength. Yet, incidentally, His words become a revelation of the nature of God. Our life and our faith are so closely connected that the saying which illuminates the one has become the foundation of the other. All creeds are based on the baptismal words: 'We must believe as we have been baptized.'[1] One fruitful word from the lips of the risen Christ has at once restored to man the life of union with God, and revealed the innermost Being of Him into whose fellowship it admits us.

The appendix to S. Mark presents the whole of these instructions in a different and probably much later and less accurate form. According to the writer of Mark xvi. 9-20 the Lord said, apparently on this occasion of the meeting among the hills, *Go ye into all the world, and preach the gospel to the whole creation.*[2] *He that believeth and is baptized shall be saved, but he that disbelieveth shall be condemned.*[3] There is nothing here which is not consistent with S. Matthew's version of the story, or with the general teaching of the New

---

[1] S. Basil, *Ep.* ii. 22 δεῖ ἡμᾶς βαπτίζεσθαι μὲν ὡς παρελάβομεν, πιστεύειν δὲ ὡς βαπτιζόμεθα.

[2] πάσῃ τῇ κτίσει.   [3] ὁ δὲ ἀπιστήσας κατακριθήσεται.

Testament. That Baptism is 'generally necessary to salvation' is taught in genuine writings of the early Apostolic age ;[1] whilst disbelief in Jesus Christ is held to be in itself the surest condemnation of the moral state of a man who, having seen the true light, turns from it.[2] Nevertheless the passage in S. Mark must be used with caution ; the words which the writer has added to the Matthaean saying may be merely an inference, although a just inference, from the original tradition, and not an actual part of the saying of Christ.

To Baptism the Lord adds another not less necessary part of the process by which the nations of the world are to be made His disciples. *Disciple all the nations . . . teaching them to keep all things whatsoever I enjoined upon you.* Instruction is to follow baptism, and the instruction of the baptized is to be based on the teaching which the Twelve had themselves received. At first sight this direction seems to contradict the teaching of the last discourse (Jo. xiv.-xvi.) ; for does not the discourse represent the earlier teaching as elementary and preparatory, and the teaching of the Spirit as that upon which the Apostles were to rely in the time to come ? *When he, the Spirit of truth, is come, he shall guide you into all the truth ;*

[1] *e.g.* Acts ii.. 38, 40 f., 47 ; Tit. iii. 5 : 1 Pet. iii. 21.

[2] Jo. iii. 18 ff., 36.

he shall teach you all things.[1] Yes, but to the
words last quoted the Lord immediately adds :
*and bring to your remembrance all that I said
unto you.* The work of the Spirit was not to
supersede the teaching of Jesus, but to interpret
and continue it. The Lord's commands, as given
to the Apostles and first disciples, and by them
transmitted through the Gospels to the Church,
remain the basis of Christian living ; to keep His
commandments is and must ever be the first
proof of true discipleship.[2] The Spirit has indeed, in the experience of the Church, guided
men into manifold ways of fulfilling the Lord's
commands ; but no principle of action which was
laid down by Him has become obsolete or un-
tenable. It is significant of the prominence which
belongs to the moral teaching of Jesus that our
own age, though ready at times to set aside the
teaching of S. Paul or S. John, holds fast by
the Sermon on the Mount. Many who regard
the Christianity of the Churches as evanescent
claim a foremost place in the religion of the
future for the Christianity which they suppose to
have been taught by Jesus Christ. The Churches
may learn from such adversaries ; they remind us
that our first duty to the world which we desire
to baptize into Christ is to enforce by word and

[1] Jo. xvi. 13, xiv. 26.   [2] Jo. xiv. 15, 21, 23.

example the lessons of purity, righteousness, truth, inwardness, and love which formed the substance of the Lord's Galilean teaching.

The great commission ends with à great promise: *Behold, I am with you always, until the consummation of the age.*[1] 'The consummation of the age' is a favourite phrase with the compiler of the first Gospel, answering, as seems to have been successfully proved, to an Aramaic equivalent, which may have been used by the Lord on each of the occasions when it occurs.[2] The conception belongs to the Jewish apocalyptic literature, which represents the present age as the last in a series of ages,[3] and as itself approaching its end or consummation. Till that end comes, till the new age[4] begins and brings new conditions of life and service, the risen Master will still be with His Church in her efforts to fulfil His last command. He will be with her 'all the days' of the intervening years or centuries as truly as He was that day when He stood on the hills above the Sea of Galilee, and sent her forth into the world. The words may have been an enigma to those who heard

[1] ἕως τῆς συντελείας τοῦ αἰῶνος.

[2] It occurs in Mt. xiii. 39, 40, 94 ; xxiv. 2 ; xxviii. 20. See Allen, *S. Matthew*, pp. 153, 254 ; and for the Aramaic equivalent, Dalman, *Words of Jesus*, p. 155.

[3] ἡ συντέλεια τῶν αἰώνων: cf. Heb. ix. 26.

[4] ὁ αἰὼν ὁ ἐρχόμενος (Mc. x. 30).

F

them spoken ; for had not the Lord said, *I ascend*, and how could He go to the Father and yet remain with His disciples on earth? And, again, what became of His promise to return at the Parousia? But events interpreted and are still interpreting the riddle ; the Lord is with us to the end in the Spirit which He has sent from the Father. Wherever the Spirit of Jesus is, there is Jesus Himself; and the Spirit came, when the Lord departed, to abide with us 'for ever,'[1] even to the consummation of the present age.

The question arises here whether the appearance by appointment to the Eleven on the high ground of Galilee is to be identified with the appearance to 'above five hundred brethren at once,' for which S. Paul vouches in 1 Cor. xv. 6. On the one hand S. Matthew speaks only of the Eleven, S. Paul, of five hundred and more ; on the other, it cannot be maintained that S. Matthew's mention of the Eleven excludes the presence of other disciples,[2] and it seems certain that an appearance to so large a body of disciples at one time could only have taken place on the Galilean hills.[3]

[1] Jo. xiv. 16, εἰς τὸν αἰῶνα.

[2] Compare *e.g.* Jo. xx. 19 ff. with Lc. xxiv. 33.

[3] Latham, p. 279 f. Mr. Latham further urges with much force (p. 291) that a meeting with the Eleven only would not have necessitated an appointment in the hill country : it could have been held with perfect safety in a room at Capernaum.

Moreover, it is not impossible that, as on Easter night, the Lord, when giving a commission to the Eleven as representative of the whole Church, would associate with them the non-official members of the brotherhood.

We can readily imagine the gathering of the five hundred ; how the call was spread throughout Galilee by willing feet, wherever the Master was known to have faithful followers ; with what secrecy it was delivered, with what eagerness received ; how on the appointed day those who received it flocked, two or three from a village, a dozen or a score from a walled town, to the appointed place upon the hills. It may have been some of these who had not seen the risen Lord hitherto, that were doubtful at first of the identity of the person who appeared to them. But if so, their doubts vanished before His words, and when S. Paul wrote his first letter to Corinth, some twenty-five years after the Resurrection, there were still more than two hundred and fifty living eye-witnesses of that day's wonder. The Apostle makes much of such a ' cloud of witnesses,' as well he might ; for even if the Eleven could be deceived or deceivers, was it credible that their error or their fraud would be shared by so great a company ? Some there must have been among them who, as the days went on, would have exposed the imposture or

betrayed their doubts.   But if any doubts of this
kind had arisen, it would have been dangerous for
the Apostle to appeal to the survivors of the
five hundred in a letter written to Corinth, where
he had enemies who were in frequent communica-
tion with Jerusalem.

Efforts have been made to set aside the evidence
of the five hundred brethren.   Renan, in his light-
hearted way of disposing of a difficulty, finds an
explanation in some fancied peculiarity of the atmosphere of the Galilean hills.[1]   A more specious
objector urges that on psychological grounds it is
permissible to believe that an illusion accepted by
the Eleven would rapidly spread through the whole
company, and overcome the rising doubts of which
S. Matthew speaks.   The few who were at first
disposed to exercise their own judgement, would
presently succumb to the entrancing hope that Jesus
was indeed risen and in their midst.   Faith, no less
than unbelief, is contagious, and the simple peasants
of the north would readily accept the opinion of
their leaders as final.   Instances are quoted of the
credulity which in certain circumstances will seize
a crowd and overpower it.   Thus, it is contended,
the witness of the five hundred resolves itself into

[1] *Les Apôtres*, p. 35 : ' L'air sur ces hauteurs est plein d'étranges
miroitements . . . Le sentiment qu'inspire le clair horizon de ces
montagnes est l'idée de l'ampleur du monde avec l'envie de le
conquérir.'

the witness of the Eleven, who were already pre-
disposed to ' see the Lord ' that day among the
hills.   But this argument assumes that the Galilean
disciples were ripe for accepting the Resurrection
of Jesus on the slightest evidence, a supposition of
which there is no proof whatever.   And it leaves
out of sight the important consideration that the
appearance on the mountain is only one of a series
of appearances, which must be weighed as a whole
and not as isolated facts.   The cumulative evidence
of the Resurrection which arises from the other
appearances is sufficient to create a strong presumption that Jesus did in some sense rise again
and shew Himself alive.   And if He rose from the
dead and appeared to the Apostles and their company at Jerusalem, it is assuredly not incredible
that on one occasion He manifested Himself to
the whole body of His Galilean followers among
the scenes of His early ministry.

VIII.

TO JAMES.

AUTHORITIES : 1 Cor. xv. 7 ; Gospel according to the Hebrews.

AFTER[1] the appearance to above five hundred brethren the Lord *appeared to James.*[2] So we learn from S. Paul, who is the only witness to the fact. The James intended is, doubtless, not the son of Zebedee who was put to death by Herod Agrippa, but the brother of the Lord, with whom S. Paul came into contact on more than one occasion,[3] and from whom he probably received an account of this manifestation. James seems to have been the eldest of the Lord's brethren. When Jesus preached at Nazareth people asked one another, *Is not this the . . . brother of James and Joses and Judas and Simon ?*[4] putting James first of the four ; and his subsequent position in the Church at Jerusalem

---

[1] ἔπειτα, 'next in order.'   [2] 1 Cor. xv. 7.

[3] Acts xv. 12 f., xxi. 18 ; Gal. i. 19, ii. 9.

[4] Mc. vi. 3 ; cf. Mt. xiii. 55.

points to the same conclusion. Thus he was the natural representative of the family of Jesus, and it may have been in this capacity that he received a separate revelation of the risen Lord. The Lord's brethren, as we know from the fourth Gospel, and might have gathered from the Synoptists,[1] did not believe in Him during the ministry, and it is unlikely that His death by crucifixion would have brought them nearer to faith.[2] Yet after the Ascension we find them consorting with the Eleven,[3] as members of the Christian brotherhood ; while at a later time James became the recognized leader of the Church at Jerusalem[4]—a 'pillar' of the Church, worthy to be named with S. Peter and S. John. It is evident that a remarkable change of attitude on the part of the relatives of Jesus took place in the interval between the Passover and the Pentecost of the year of the Crucifixion. Such a change can only have been due to the belief that He had risen from the dead, and had thus proved Himself to be the Messiah. It may well have been with a view to bring about this conviction that the Lord showed Himself separately to His eldest brother. If so, it is easy to under-

[1] Jo. vii. 5 ; cf. Mc. iii. 32.

[2] See Lightfoot, *Galatians*, p. 265 ; Mayor, *S. James*, p. xlv, argues against this view, but not, as it seems to me, successfully.

[3] Acts. i. 14.   [4] Acts. xii. 17, xv. 13, xxi. 18 ; Gal. ii. 9, 12.

stand the special interest which this appearance to
James had for S. Paul. It had changed the course
of James's life, just as S. Paul's had been changed
by the vision on the way to Damascus. In each
case the reality of the manifestation had been
proved, in the experience of the eye-witness, by
its abiding results.

S. Paul says nothing as to the nature of the
interview that passed between James and his Divine
Brother. It does not fall in with the purpose of
his summary in I Cor. xv. to enter into details.
But it may be doubted whether in this instance
he knew more than he has told us. As in the
case of the Easter Day appearance to S. Peter,
the words that fell from the Lord may have
seemed to James too personal to be communicated
even to a brother disciple. When Saul, three years
after his conversion, went up to Jerusalem to visit
Cephas, and met James also, he doubtless told
them how he had seen the Lord on the way to
Damascus. It is easy to imagine how the others
would add their own experiences, Peter saying,
'He appeared to me also, on the day that He
rose,' and James, 'And to me also afterwards.'
Each would be full of his own thoughts, but
neither would care to lift the veil any further,
and Saul on his part would have shrunk from
asking for confidences which were not offered.

The Gospel according to the Hebrews, however, has an anecdote of the appearance to James which must be given for what it is worth. ' The Lord went to James and appeared to him ; for James had sworn that he would not eat bread from the hour in which he had drunk the cup of the Lord until he saw Him rising from the dead. . . . *Bring*, the Lord said, *a table and bread* . . . He brought bread, and [Jesus] blessed and brake it and gave it to James the Just, and said to him, *My brother, eat thy bread, for the Son of Man has risen from the dead.*'[1] To this story the objection at once presents itself that the Lord's brother was not, so far as we know, present at the first Eucharist, so that if the incident has any foundation in fact it must relate to James the son of Zebedee, and not to James the Just. Bishop Lightfoot, indeed, meets this difficulty by reading ' in which the Lord[2] had drunk His cup,' *i.e.* the cup of suffering referred to in Mark x. 38 f. But the story in either form presupposes that James was already a believer in Jesus before His death, of which there is no other evidence. On the whole, though it is both early and not in

[1] This is from Jerome's Latin rendering of the Hebrew Gospel (*de Viris illustr*. 2).

[2] The Greek version of the story has Κύριος. See Lightfoot, *Galatians*, p. 274.

itself improbable,[1] this account of the Lord's interview with James cannot with any confidence be connected with the appearance to James the Lord's brother of which S. Paul speaks.

[1] See Mayor, *S. James*, p. xxxvii.

IX.

TO THE ELEVEN, BEFORE ASCENDING.

AUTHORITIES: 'Mc.' xvi. 19-20; Lc. xxiv. 44 (?)-52; Acts i. 4 (?)-11;
1 Cor. xv. 7.

THE appearance to James, the Lord's brother, was
followed, as S. Paul tells us, by an appearance 'to
all the Apostles,'[1] *i.e.* to the Apostles as a body,
the Eleven assembled in one place. Since S. Paul's
own experience on the Damascus road is mentioned
immediately afterwards, this appearance to the
Eleven may be taken to be the final interview, or
group of interviews, before the Ascension, of which
we have some account in the third Gospel and the
Acts.

S. Luke, who, as we have seen, takes no notice
of the return of the Eleven to Galilee after the
Passover, distinctly places the last scenes in
Jerusalem and its neighbourhood. His omission
of the appearances in Galilee is more than dis-
counted by the narratives of S. Matthew (who in

---

[1] 1 Cor. xv. 7 εἶτα τοῖς ἀποστόλοις πᾶσιν.

all probability followed S. Mark) and S. John ;
but his positive evidence remains unshaken, and it
compels us to suppose that the fifth or sixth week
after the Passover saw the Apostles and their party
again in Judaea. We are left in ignorance of the
reason for their return to the south ; it was scarcely
the approach of the Pentecost which brought them
back to Jerusalem, for the Pentecost was at least
a week after the Ascension.[1] Possibly as their
steps had been guided to Galilee, so now they
were directed by the Lord to return to Jerusalem;
'there,' He may have said at the last interview in
Galilee, 'ye shall see me again.'[2] While Galilee,
with its associations and its comparative security,
was admirably fitted for the manifestations which
were vouchsafed there, Jerusalem was the destined
scene of the beginnings of the Church's life and
work,[3] and it was in the neighbourhood of Jerusalem
that the last events of the forty days must take
place.

If we suppose the Eleven to have spent a fortnight in Galilee, it was still possible for them to
be at Jerusalem again at the end of the fifth week

[1] Even if we accepted the statement of the Ep. of Barnabas (§ 15,
ad fin.) that the Ascension took place on the first day of the week.

[2] Renan's explanation (*Les Apôtres*, p. 45 : ' Le retour à Jérusalem
fut donc résolu par ceux qui à ce moment dirigeaient la secte ')
presupposes an organization which at the time did not exist.

[3] Lc. xxiv. 47, Acts i. 4, 8.

after Easter. We will think of them as once more assembled at Jerusalem in the large upper room where they had met on the night of the Resurrection Day. It is the first day of the sixth week since the Passover ;[1] the hour is late and the doors are shut. Once more Jesus stands in the midst. But there is now no panic, scarcely any surprise ; such appearances had grown familiar, and it may be that on this occasion, as once or twice before, the day and the place had been determined beforehand.

In S. Luke's compressed narratives there are only faint marks [2] of any break in the series of teachings which began on Easter night. In these circumstances opinions naturally differ as to the arrangement of the materials. Let us suppose that Luke xxiv. 44-46 or 47 belongs to the Sunday before the Ascension and the rest to the day of the Ascension. On this assumption the earlier instruction turns on two points : the fulfilment of the Old Testament in the passion and resurrection of the Christ ; the carrying out of the purpose of the New Covenant

[1] This is of course purely conjectural. But it is clear from Lc. xxiv. 50, 52, Acts i. 12 that the final instructions began in Jerusalem and ended on the Mount of Olives; and the nature of the instructions as they are sketched in S. Luke's two accounts suggests that more than one interview must have taken place.

[2] εἶπεν δὲ αὐτοῖς (v. 44), καὶ εἶπεν αὐτοῖς (v. 46). Cf. Acts i. 4 συναλιζόμενος παρήγγειλεν αὐτοῖς, ib. 6 οἱ μὲν οὖν συνελθόντες ἠρώτων αὐτόν.

in the preaching of the future Church. Of the
former of these the Lord had already spoken to
the disciples on the way to Emmaus; but the
Eleven had not heard what was then said, and for
them as Jews, starting from the basis of the older
covenant, the point was vital. Not that it was
altogether new to them, for the Lord had often
during His ministry called their attention to it.
*These are my words which I spake unto you
while I was yet with you,*[1] *how that all things
must needs be fulfilled which are written in the
law of Moses and the prophets and the psalms,
concerning me.* But they had but ill understood the lesson, and now He insisted upon it
at length. He shewed them that the Law, the
Prophets, and Psalms,[2] all found their ultimate
explanation in the Gospel of the Incarnation. All
presupposed the coming of a Christ such as Jesus
was, a Christ who should suffer, die, rise again, and
through whom a gospel of reconciliation could be
preached to all mankind. The system of outward
purifications and material sacrifices provided by the
Law of Moses is intelligible only when it is regarded
as propaedeutic ; the Law fulfilled its purpose by

[1] See *e.g.* Jo. v. 46.

[2] Unless the ' Psalms ' here represent the Hagiographa, which is
unlikely, they are singled out from the third division of the Hebrew
canon as being so largely conversant with the Messianic hope.

serving as a tutor who brought men to the school of Christ.[1]   Similarly the Prophets and the Psalmists raised expectations and created ideals, which ought to have prepared the Jewish people for such a Messiah as Jesus, and such a reign of righteousness and truth as He preached to the world.   That the Old Testament had not done this, that the nation as a whole had rejected its King, that even the followers of Jesus and the Apostles themselves had failed to understand the nature of His Kingdom, was due to a misconception.   They had interpreted the Law, the Prophets, and the Psalms amiss ; they had judged their national scriptures according to the letter, not according to the spirit.   The teachers of the new Israel must shake themselves free from this error, and the Lord gave them now their first lesson in this new learning ; He *opened their mind that they might understand the Scriptures.   Thus it is written*, He said, *that the Christ should suffer and rise again from the dead on the third day ; and that repentance and remission of sins should be preached in his name*[2] *unto all the nations.*   The Old Testament, rightly understood, had not only foreshadowed the Passion and Resurrection of the Messiah ; it had anticipated the extension of the covenant to the

---

[1] Gal. iii. 24 ὁ νόμος παιδαγωγὸς ἡμῶν γέγονεν εἰς Χριστόν.

[2] ἐπὶ τῷ ὀνόματι αὐτοῦ = on the basis of faith in His Messianic character and work.

whole Gentile world. The Psalmists and Prophets in particular had foreseen that in the days of the Messiah the world would be called to repentance, and receive through repentance and faith in His Name the remission of sins. All the wonders that had come to pass in the eventful years of the ministry, all the unknown events that lay before the Church in the evangelization of the world, were already present in that great scheme of things for which the Old Testament was preparatory ; all were contained in the Law, the Prophets, and the Psalms as the leaves and flower and fruit are already in the seed, as the forest tree is in the sapling, or the adult is in the infant. The future would be an outgrowth of the past ; the Church as she rose to her great task of regenerating the world would but carry to their goal the yearnings and preparations of ancient Israel.

That one great lesson, with its double aim, its retrospect, and its outlook on the future, must surely have sufficed for the first meeting after the return to Jerusalem. To a second meeting, which began in the upper room and ended on the hill of the Ascension, may perhaps be attributed the rest of the teaching in the last chapter of S. Luke's Gospel and the first chapter of the Acts.[1] Again the Lord stood in the midst, or perhaps He sat

[1] Lc. xxiv. 47^b-49, Acts i. 4-8.

at table [1] with the Eleven as with the two disciples at Emmaus. At this last interview His thoughts would naturally be directed to the immediate future of the Eleven and the Church. He was on the point of departure, and some days must intervene before the coming of the Other Paraclete. The interval was perhaps a necessary trial of faith and patience. It was to be a time of waiting and not of action, and meanwhile they were to stay where they were. Their preaching was to begin from Jerusalem,[2] and the descent of the Spirit must find them there. *He charged them not to depart from Jerusalem, but to wait for the promise of the Father, which, said he, ye heard from me.*[3] *Behold, I send forth the promise of my Father upon you, but tarry ye in the city until ye be clothed with power from on high.*[4] *John indeed baptized with water, but ye shall be baptized with the Holy Spirit not many days hence.*[5]

Perhaps the words 'clothed with power from on high' suggested to the still undeveloped minds of the Eleven the hope of some visible manifestation of glory which would array them in shining garments, as Jesus was arrayed on the Mount of

---

[1] συναλιζόμενος (Acts i. 4) has been thought by many modern commentators to imply this: see Knowling, *ad loc.*

[2] Lc. ἀρξάμενοι ἀπὸ Ἰερουσαλήμ.   [3] Acts i. 4.

[4] Lc. xxiv. 49. The 'I' is emphatic (ἐγὼ ἀποστέλλω): cf. Jo. xv. 26 ὃν ἐγὼ πέμψω ὑμῖν παρὰ τοῦ πατρός.

[5] Acts i. 5.

Transfiguration, and bring the enemies of the
Master, Roman and Jewish, to their knees.
Certainly their old hopes of Messianic splendour
sprang to life again, and one of them—was it
Peter, or James the son of Zebedee, or Simon the
Zealot?—ventured to ask, *Lord, dost thou at this
time restore the kingdom to Israel?*[1] This, after
all the light thrown upon the Old Testament at
their last meeting with Him! It was vain to
insist any further upon the spiritual nature of the
Divine Kingdom, or the meaning of 'Israel' in
the new economy, until the Spirit came and led
them by new ways into the fuller truth.[2] All
that could be done now was to turn the thoughts
of the Eleven from useless speculation to the great
work that lay before them. *It is not for you*,
the Lord answered, *to know times or seasons*—the
exact day and hour, or even the opportune epoch
for the manifestation of the Kingdom of God : all
such matters belong to the secret counsels of the
Father ; they are reserved for His own determination, and do not belong to the field of human
knowledge ;[3] *the Father hath set* them *within his
own authority*, and to inquire about this is to
invade a Divine privilege. What concerns you
to know at present is that you are to receive
power to fulfil the work committed to you. *Ye*

[1] Acts i. 6.   [2] Jo. xvi. 13 ὁδηγήσει ὑμᾶς.   [3] Cf. Mc. xiii. 32.

shall receive power when the Holy Ghost is come upon you, and ye shall be my witnesses.[1]

Of the Paraclete the Lord had said on the night before the Passion, *He shall bear witness of me* ; adding, *and ye also bear witness, because ye have been with me from the beginning.*[2] The Spirit was to bear His witness with and through the Apostles, He strengthening and guiding them to do their part, they co-operating with Him by word and deed, bearing their testimony to the things which they had heard and seen, as the Spirit gave them utterance ; they preaching the Gospel of the Christ, He carrying their words with conviction[3] to the hearts of men. In an especial manner the first preaching of the Gospel must be of the nature of personal testimony borne by eye- and ear-witnesses. *That which we have heard,* writes S. John to the men of the next generation, *that which we have seen with our eyes, that which we beheld and our hands handled concerning the Word of life . . . that which we have seen and heard declare we unto you.*[4] No words could better describe the general character of the Apostolic preaching.[5] But for this work of bearing

---

[1] Acts i. 8 ; cf. Lc. xxiv. 48. [2] Jo. xv. 26 f.

[3] Jo. xvi. 8. ἐλέγξει τὸν κόσμον. [4] 1 Jo. i. 2 f.

[5] According to a very early tradition the simple and descriptive Gospel of S. Mark is based on the preaching of S. Peter at Rome.

witness of things which had come within their
own knowledge little was needed beyond a memory
quickened by the Spirit of Jesus Christ and a
courage to speak in the presence of men of all
sorts and conditions with absolute fearlessness and
truth.   Such 'freedom of speech'[1] was   assured
to them by the presence in their lives of the
Holy Ghost.

The work was to proceed in an orderly manner ;
beginning from Jerusalem,[2] the capital of the old
theocracy, the scene of the Passion and Resurrection
of the Lord, they were gradually to enlarge the
scope of their preaching till it was co-extensive with
the world : *ye shall be my witnesses both in Jerusalem,
and in all Judaea and Samaria, and unto the utter-
most part of the earth.*   The message was to be
carried from Jerusalem through the towns and
villages of Judaea, thence northwards to Samaria,
which even in the early days of the ministry was
ripening for the harvest,[3] and from Samaria to
the lands which were frankly heathen.   Galilee is
omitted, for Galilee had already had its opportunity, and there were more than five hundred
brethren there who had 'seen the Lord,' and to
whom the work of bearing witness might be left.

If it is asked how far this programme was

[1] παρρησία : cf. Acts ii. 29 ; iv. 13, 29, 31.
[2] Lc. xxiv. 47.   [3] Jo. iv. 35.

actually carried out by the original Eleven, the answer must be that we do not know. The Acts shew that S. Peter and S. John preached in Jerusalem, and S. Peter throughout Judaea, and that both Apostles afterwards strengthened the work of Philip the evangelist in Samaria. S. Peter also subsequently went down to Antioch, and an early and scarcely doubtful tradition carries him to Rome. Of the other nine members of the original Apostolate James the son of Zebedee suffered under Herod Agrippa I.; the rest seem afterwards to have left Jerusalem and gone their several ways. A comparatively late story represents them as dividing the world between them for the purpose of evangelization ; and Eusebius knew of a tradition that Scythia was allotted to Andrew, Parthia to Thomas, India to Bartholomew.[1] But no reliance can be placed upon these details, and it may be that at least the greater number of the Apostles never carried their message beyond Syria or Asia Minor. Yet if they did not personally fulfil the Lord's last charge, yet by their witness in Jerusalem they at least prepared the way for others to do so. Even S. Paul, in the full consciousness of his own great office as the Apostle of the

[1] Eusebius, *H.E.* iii. 1 : Θωμᾶς μέν, ὡς ἡ παράδοσις περιέχει, τὴν Παρθίαν εἴληχεν, Ἀνδρέας δὲ τὴν Σκυθίαν, Ἰωάννης τὴν Ἀσίαν. Cf. Harnack, *Expansion of Christianity*, i. p. 84 f., 438 f. ; the evidence is collected in ii. p. 147 ff.

Gentiles, recognizes the great position assigned
to Apostles in the foundation of the universal
Church.[1]   Moreover, the Lord's words, though
addressed immediately to the Eleven, did not
exhaust themselves in the work of the first generation.   The command to bear witness to the Christ is
in varying circumstances fulfilled by each generation,
as it serves the counsel of God.   The original
witnesses broke the ground, and started the cam-
paign ; succeeding ages of the Church have taken
up their work, and in the power of the same Spirit
have borne their testimony to the Christ.

The last interview of the risen Lord with the
Eleven began in Jerusalem, probably in the upper
room, which they seem to have secured as their
place of meeting.[2]   But it did not end there.   As
on the night before the Passion in the midst of
His discourse the Lord had said, 'Arise, let us go
hence,' and so saying had led the disciples out of
the city towards the Mount of Olives ; so now, we
must suppose, at some point in the conversation
which has not been indicated, He rose, and followed
by the Eleven, went through the streets of Jerusalem
for the last time, passed through the Eastern gate,
and crossed the Kidron valley.   But on this occasion

[1] Eph. ii. 20 ; cf. Rev. xxi. 14.

[2] Acts i. 13 τὸ ὑπερῷον . . . οὗ ἦσαν καταμένοντες.   On the site
of the *Cenaculum* see Sanday, *Sacred Sites*, p. 77 ff. and plates xlviii.-l.

He did not stop at Gethsemane, but passed on in
the direction of Bethany. *He led them out until they
were over against Bethany.*[1] So S. Luke tells us in
his Gospel; in the Acts he makes the Apostles
return after the Ascension *from the mount called
Olivet, which is nigh unto Jerusalem, a Sabbath day's
journey off,* i.e. at a distance of five or six furlongs,
less than three-quarters of an English mile. But
the village of Bethany lies in a hollow on the
east slope of Olivet, more than twice as far from
the city. Even if the distances agreed, it could not
be supposed that the last scene took place in or
near habitations. The traditional site is on the
summit of the central height of the Mount of
Olives, a position too near to Jerusalem and in
full view of the city.[2] We must think rather of
some place on or near the Bethany road, about
half way between Bethany and Jerusalem, suffi-
ciently remote from both and yet within sight of
the former at least. Such a spot was noted by the
writer of these pages during a visit to Palestine in
1869, and there may be others which satisfy the
conditions described by S. Luke.

At some such place on the hillside the Lord

[1] So R.V. rightly translates ἕως πρὸς Βηθανίαν, *i.e.* 'until (they came
to be where they were looking) towards B.' Bethany is now
el 'Azariyeh.

[2] See Stanley (*Sinai and Palestine*, p. 452 ff.), who remarks upon
'the almost offensive publicity of the traditional spot.'

halted, and the Eleven with Him. There we
may believe Him to have spoken at least the last
words about the witness to be borne by the
Eleven in the power of the promised Spirit. When
the final instruction had been given, He lifted up
the pierced hands, after the manner of a priest
giving benediction, and blessed them, and in the
very act of blessing, He was separated from them.[1]
He withdrew Himself, passed into the invisible,
as on many previous occasions since the Ascension.
But there was a special feature in this withdrawal
which marked it as different from the rest, for as
S. Luke adds in his second treatise, the Lord
was now *lifted up*, and as His feet were seen to
rise from the ground, a low cloud, coming up
from the Mediterranean, swept the side of the
hill, wrapt Him round,[2] and then sailed away
eastward and upward, as if it were carrying Him
to heaven.[3] Ever afterwards the Church spoke of
this last disappearance as an 'assumption'[4] or an
'ascension,'[5] and under this name the event took
its place as an article of faith in the earliest
creeds ; 'He ascended into heaven' stands already

---

[1] Lc. ἐν τῷ εὐλογεῖν αὐτοὺς διέστη ἀπ' αὐτῶν.   [2] ὑπέλαβεν αὐτόν.

[3] See Lc. xxiv. 51 where codd. ℵ and D add καὶ ἀνεφέρετο εἰς
τὸν οὐρανόν.   1 Pet. iii. 22 πορευθεὶς εἰς οὐρανόν.

[4] ἀνάλημψις (Acts i. 2, 11, 22 ; 1 Tim. iii. 16 ; 'Mc.' xvi. 19).

[5] ἀνάβασις (Jo. xx. 17, Eph. iv. 8 ff.).

in the old Roman creed of the second century, as it stands in our ' Apostles' Creed ' to-day.[1]

The Ascension presents to many minds to-day a difficulty even greater than the Resurrection. It seems to conflict with even an elementary knowledge of physics. Is it to be believed that in defiance of the laws of Nature[2] the Lord's human body rose through the air till He reached the bounds of the earth's atmosphere, and then passing through the spaces of the universe attained by this process of physical translation to the immediate Presence of the Infinite Life ? Such a way of conceiving the Ascension is at once a misreading of the historical fact, and a misapprehension of the inner truth which it represents. It is a fact, as we believe, that forty days more or less[3] after the Resurrection the Lord finally withdrew His risen body from the eyes and touch of His disciples, and that in the moment of His disappearance He was enveloped by a passing cloud, which travelled upwards as if it were carrying Him up to heaven. And this fact was the symbol of a great and vital Christian truth, which is also a fact, but in the spiritual world.

---

[1] See the writer's *Apostles' Creed*, p. 64 ff.

[2] This expression was used quite recently by a preacher in the writer's hearing.

[3] δι' ἡμερῶν τεσσεράκοντα ὀπτανόμενος (Acts i. 3).

The risen Lord has crowned His victory over death by passing in His spiritual body into the invisible order, by returning to the Father who is above all. The mind naturally connects that higher life which is beyond our present comprehension with the blue heights that are above us, or the starry heavens which seem to be above the blue, or with some imaginary elevation to that which is beyond the stars. In condescension to this weakness we are permitted to think of our Lord as having 'ascended into the heavens,' or as the writer to the Hebrews expresses the same truth, having *passed through the heavens*.[1]   He has passed out of our present sphere of being into one which is beyond the furthest limits that we can conceive, higher than the highest heavens are above the earth, and yet (it may be) nearer to us than the nearest object in the physical world. His Ascension was, in fact, the last of the withdrawals which followed the appearances of the forty days; a withdrawal which ended, till the consummation of the age, His visible presence on this earth. But it did not end—rather it began—His promised presence with us in the Spirit. He is *at the right hand of God*,[2] in the highest region to which

---

[1] Heb. iv. 14 διεληλυθότα τοὺς οὐρανούς.

[2] Rom. viii. 34, Eph. i. 20, Col. iii. 1, Heb. i. 3, 1 Pet. iii. 22, 'Mc.' xvi. 19.

human nature can attain ; and yet behind the thin veil of phenomena, He is still in our midst. Any view of the Ascension which locates our Lord's presence in some distant world leaves out of sight one of the most important purposes of His exalted life—its direct action upon the living Church in her successive generations to the end of time. We have His word that whatever His departure to the Father and elevation to heaven may mean, He has not been parted from His brethren on earth even for a time.[1]

According to S. Luke's second account in the Acts, the Ascension was followed by a vision of angels.[2] It is surprising that we hear so little of the intervention of angels in the events of the forty days. They appear only at the beginning and at the end, to announce the Resurrection, and to explain the Ascension. A fictitious narrative of the manifestations of the risen Christ would probably have brought an angelic choir or retinue into the scene on almost every occasion when He appeared.[3] The simple record of fact which satisfies the Evangelists, introduces angels only when angels are necessary. The Eleven who witnessed the

[1] The Ascension has even brought Him into closer contact with them (Jo. xx. 27 ; see p. 8 f.).

[2] Acts i. 10 f.

[3] Especially in view of such a saying as we find in Jo. i. 51.

Ascension were unable to interpret it ; it was hard for them to believe that this was indeed the return to the Father of which the Lord had spoken, and His final withdrawal from the sight of men. Their eyes followed the cloud, not perhaps without an expectation that the Lord would presently re-appear. *While they were looking stedfastly into heaven as he went up, behold, two men stood by them in white apparel, which also said, Ye men of Galilee, why stand ye looking into heaven? this Jesus which was received up from you into heaven shall so come in like manner as ye beheld him going into heaven.*

So the Eleven realized at length that for the present at least no fresh manifestation must be expected. When it came, it would be, as it were, a reversal of the Ascension, a descent from heaven, not a mere reappearance in the upper room, by the sea, or on the Galilean hills, but a revealed Presence[1] such as would change the living and raise the dead. For this last Epiphany[2] they continued to look, clinging for a generation or two to the belief that it might come within the limit of their own lives, and leaving to the future Church the

[1] παρουσία, Mt. xxiv. 3, 1 Cor. xv. 23, 1 Th. ii. 19, Jas. v. 7, 1 Jo. ii. 28.

[2] ἐπιφάνεια, 2 Th. ii. 8 ; 1 Tim. vi. 14 ; 2 Tim. i. 10 ; iv. 1, 8 ; Tit. ii. 13.

inspiration of a great hope, which, as we believe, will be realized in days yet to come, although far otherwise than as they supposed.[1] The Departure implies a Return, the withdrawal a reappearance. Even the last disappearance that ended the great Forty Days was not final. There is a greater Vision in store ; *we shall see him even as he is.*[2]

[1] Cf. Westcott, *Gospel of the Resurrection*, p. 128 ff.
[2] 1 Jo. iii. 2.

APPEARANCES AFTER THE
ASCENSION.

THOU SITTEST AT THE RIGHT HAND OF GOD,
IN THE GLORY OF THE FATHER.
WE BELIEVE THAT THOU SHALT COME
TO BE OUR JUDGE.
WE THEREFORE PRAY THEE, HELP
THY SERVANTS.

I.

TO STEPHEN.

AUTHORITY: Acts vii. 55, 56.

THE Ascension ended the appearances of the risen Lord of which cognizance could be taken by the senses. But visions of the ascended Christ were seen on several occasions until the end of the century. Some of these are described in the Acts and later books of the New Testament, and they deserve careful study.

In Jerusalem, after the coming of the Holy Spirit, the new society grew by leaps and bounds.[1] Some six years had passed since the Crucifixion, and though as yet no uncircumcised Gentile had found his way into the Church, both the great sections of the Jewish people were represented among its members, the Aramaic-speaking Jews of Palestine,[2] and the Greek-speaking Jews,[3] who came for the most part from Egypt and Asia Minor, or from the Greek cities of Syria. The

[1] See Acts i. 15; ii. 41, 47; iv. 4; v. 14; vi. 1, 7.
[2] Ἑβραῖοι.   [3] Ἑλληνισταί.

differences of language and general tone which they brought into the Christian brotherhood led to heartburnings which threatened dissension ; there were rumours of partiality being shewn by the Eleven towards the Aramaic-speaking brethren, to the neglect of such as were Hellenists. The situation was wisely met by the appointment of seven brethren, elected by the whole body, to superintend the administration in reference to which the complaints had been made. It was merely a question connected with the relief of the poorer members of the Church, needing practical ability, fairness, and good judgement, rather than spiritual discernment or power.[1] Yet one at least of the seven possessed the highest spiritual gifts,[2] which, added to his official position, placed him at once in the forefront of the fierce battle which had begun between the traditionalists and the men of the new faith. Himself probably a Hellenist, Stephen encountered the special hostility of the non-Christian Hellenists in Jerusalem. Among the many synagogues of the Holy City was one[3] which consisted of freedmen partly from

[1] A διακονία τραπεζῶν rather than a διακονία τοῦ λόγου (Acts vi. 2, 4).

[2] Stephen was 'full of faith and Holy Spirit' (Acts vi. 5), 'of grace and power' (vi. 8); his speech was marked by 'wisdom and Spirit' (vi. 10), and his spiritual energy manifested itself in 'wonders and signs' (vi. 8).

[3] See Hort, *Judaistic Christianity*, p. 50.

Cyrene and Egypt, partly from Cilicia and the
province of Asia. Stephen, who may have belonged to this body, argued only too convincingly
against their narrow views of the Old Testament
and the Jewish polity. Unable to answer him,
they had recourse to the charge of blasphemy
which in Jewish circles was always at hand to
crush an inconvenient adversary. A case was got
up, witnesses were procured,[1] the passions of the
Jewish mob were roused, and Stephen was seized
and brought before the Sanhedrin, as his Master
had been, to answer for his teaching. He was
continually speaking,[2] the witnesses said, against
the Temple and the Law; they themselves had
heard him say that Jesus the Nazarene would
destroy the Temple and change the whole Mosaic
system. Stephen, called by the High Priest to
make his defence,[3] claimed that Moses himself
and the Prophets were on his side. Had not the
Prophets spoken of a greater sanctuary, and denied
that a 'house of this building' could be in the
fullest sense the dwelling place of God? Had
not Moses, though in his own day he was a 'ruler
and redeemer'[4] in Israel, and one who gave to
Israel 'living oracles,' words quick with a Divine

---

[1] ὑπέβαλον ἄνδρας (vi. 11); ἔστησαν μάρτυρας ψευδεῖς (ib. 13).

[2] οὐ παύεται λαλῶν.   [3] Acts vii. 1 ff.

[4] ἄρχοντα καὶ λυτρωτήν.

inspiration, pointed to a Prophet like unto himself, another Lawgiver, another giver of living words, to whom Israel must hearken? This new Moses, this greater Lawgiver and Prophet had come, and the men of that generation had rejected Him as their fathers rejected the mediator of the Old Covenant; had betrayed and murdered him,[1] as the prophets who foretold His coming had been murdered.

It was an answer full of Divine courage, worthy of a servant of Jesus of Nazareth. The words of Stephen cut their way like a saw through the hearts of his accusers,[2] till they ground their teeth with helpless rage. The position of the first Christian who witnessed for Christ at the cost of his life was strikingly similar to that which the Master Himself had occupied at His trial before Caiaphas. Stephen stood before the same court, and doubtless before some of the same judges; the charge was on both occasions one of blasphemy; the truth was confessed on both with equal fearlessness. He had followed the Lord to judgement, and was about to follow Him to death, the forerunner of the noble army of Christian martyrs. Was he to receive no signal support in his hour of dire need? no special token of approval from behind the veil?

---

[1] οὗ νῦν ὑμεῖς προδόται καὶ φονεῖς ἐγένεσθε.

[2] διεπρίοντο ταῖς καρδίαις αὐτῶν, καὶ ἔβρυχον τοὺς ὀδόντας ἐπ' αὐτόν.

The occasion was unique, and it was met by a unique revelation of the invisible. Stephen, *being full of the Holy Ghost, looked up stedfastly into heaven, and saw the glory of God, and Jesus standing on the right hand of God, and said, Behold I see the heaven opened and the Son of Man standing on the right hand of God.*[1] The amazing words, spoken with full conviction by one whose face was like an angel's[2] for spiritual beauty and penetration, must have reminded some who were present of the words of Jesus when He stood before the same assembly. *Ye shall see the Son of Man sitting at the right hand of power and coming with the clouds of heaven.*[3] In Stephen's vision the first part of this prophecy was seen to be already accomplished. The eternal doors had been flung open before the martyr's spirit, and his eyes had seen the King, the Lord of hosts, sitting upon a throne, high and lifted up,[4] and lo! on the right hand of the Divine Majesty was One in human form, the Son of Man who had been crucified. The picture of the exalted Christ on the right hand of God is not uncommon in the New Testament,[5] but there is one feature in Stephen's representation of it which is not repeated. Elsewhere Jesus sits on the throne, as

---

[1] Acts vii. 55 f.   [2] Acts vi. 15.   [3] Mc. xiv. 62.
[4] Cf. Isa. vi. 1, 5.   [5] See p. 106.

the Assessor of God: here only He stands at
the Father's side. He has risen from His seat
to succour His servant in the hour of great need.[1]
At the moment He is the High Priest and the
Advocate with the Father rather than the Divine
King; He stands ready to undertake Stephen's cause.

The reality of the vision in the sphere of
Stephen's own spirit is attested by its effect upon his
conduct in the catastrophe that immediately followed.
In the Council there was instantly a wild uproar;
his last words were drowned in shouts of execration;
forgetting their character of judges, regardless of
the Roman's refusal to allow them the right of
putting any man to death,[2] as one man[3] they
fell upon him, dragging him beyond the gates of
the city to the place where he was to be stoned
as a blasphemer. In that raging sea of human
passions Stephen alone remained unmoved. The
vision of the Divine Master was still upon his
spirit, and as the stones flew, he spoke only to
Him: *Lord Jesus, receive my spirit*; *Lord, lay not
this sin to their charge.*

What Stephen saw sustained him in the supreme
moment of life, and made him *more than conqueror*[4]

---

[1] Cf. Heb. iv. 16 εἰς εὔκαιρον βοήθειαν. S. Chrysostom in Cramer,
iii. p. 128: τί οὖν ἑστῶτα καὶ οὐ καθήμενον; ἵνα δείξῃ τὴν ἀντίληψιν
τὴν εἰς τὸν μάρτυρα.

[2] Jo. xviii. 31.   [3] ὁμοθυμαδόν.   [4] Rom. viii. 37 ὑπερνικῶμεν.

in death. To him it was a reality in the highest sense : more real than the yells or stones of his murderers. Was it real also in the sense that it represented actualities ? So Christians have every right to believe. That beyond the veil of sense there exists an Infinite Presence in which the human Christ who suffered and rose again lives, and from which He succours souls that call upon Him in their time of need, is a faith which con-quered the world in the first century, and will continue to conquer it till the end of time. All life is transfigured for those who believe what Stephen believed, and as he believed it.

II.

TO SAUL.

AUTHORITIES : (1) Acts ix. 3-9, xxii. 5-11, xxvi. 12-16 ; 1 Cor. ix. 1, xv. 8.
        (2) Acts xviii. 9 f.
        (3) Acts xxii. 17-21.
        (4) 2 Cor. xii. 1-9.

THE members of the Sanhedrin before whom
Stephen stood did not share his vision. Even
during the forty days spent on earth after His
Resurrection the Lord had not shewn Himself alive
to any declared enemy. Neither Pilate nor Herod,
Antipas nor Caiaphas had been permitted to receive
ocular proof that He had risen ; *to him that hath
shall be given*, but not to him that through his own
deliberate refusal of the gift hath not. Yet on one
occasion after the Ascension the Lord appeared to
a foe, and the most zealous foe that the Gospel
ever had.

Saul had taken a leading part in the judicial
murder of Stephen. Probably he had heard his
defence and his words about seeing Jesus at the
right hand of God. This overt blasphemy, as he

deemed it, thrown in the faces of the High Priest
and the other leaders of Israel, stung him to mad-
ness; he gave his approval [1] to the course which was
taken by keeping charge of the outer clothing which
the witnesses stripped off in order to cast the first
stones at the blasphemer.[2] It was Saul who followed
up the death of Stephen by searching the private
houses of Jerusalem for Christians and handing over
those he found into the safe keeping of the officers
of the Sanhedrin; [3] and it was Saul who, when
Jerusalem offered no further scope for his ravages,[4]
went to the Sanhedrin and demanded letters from
the High Priest to the synagogue of Damascus
authorizing the arrest of any Jewish disciples of
'the Way' who might be there.[5] His policy was
to stamp out the movement in Palestine and Syria
before it could penetrate to the Dispersion in east
or west ; and such was his zeal and his personal
strength that he seemed only too likely to succeed.

Saul was already near the northern capital when
his career was arrested by the vision of the ascended

[1] ἦν συνευδοκῶν (Acts viii. 1, xxii. 20).

[2] According to the law of Deut. xvii. 7. See Acts vii. 58,
xxii. 20.

[3] Acts viii. 3.

[4] ἐλυμαίνετο : cf. Gal. i. 23 ἐπόρθει.

[5] The Jewish colony at Damascus was so large that Josephus
speaks of 10,000 or even 18,000 Jews being slain there at the
breaking out of the war with Rome (Schürer, *History of the Jewish
People*, E. tr. II. i. p. 98).

Christ. There is not the faintest indication that he was seized by remorse, or even haunted by a suspicion that he was fighting against the truth. He was still, to all appearance, a convinced unbeliever down to the moment when the vision changed his life. His conversion, with its immense consequences, was due, as he himself believed and constantly affirmed, simply to what he had seen and heard ; it was the direct result of a revelation of the ascended Christ.

It is a happy circumstance that in the Acts we possess three separate and to some extent independent accounts of this momentous event. One is by the author of the book ;[1] the other two are attributed by him to S. Paul.[2] If the reader will be at the pains to write these narratives in parallel columns and compare them together, he will be rewarded by some interesting results. The first will be found to be a plain statement of the facts, without a superfluous word ; the second, which purports to be part of S. Paul's defence of himself before a Jerusalem mob, agrees closely with the first, only amplifying it here and there as one would be likely to do who told his own story in circumstances of strong excitement ; the third, which belongs to the Apostle's *apologia pro vita sua*[3] before Festus and

---

[1] Acts ix. 3-8.   [2] Acts xxii. 6-11, xxvi. 12 ff.

[3] μέλλων σήμερον ἀπολογεῖσθαι (Acts xxvi. 2 ; cf. *v.* 24).

Agrippa in the *auditorium* [1] at Caesarea, shews every sign of careful preparation, such as the same man would give to his story when he was called to deliver it before a select and impartial audience. It may be fairly assumed that these two reports are substantially correct ; it is not improbable that the historian of the Acts was present on both occasions, and it is practically certain that he had opportunities of submitting to S. Paul his drafts of both speeches before they were used for his book. We may therefore safely use them to supplement his own account, which is probably a summary of what he had learnt about the conversion from the Apostle himself.[2]

Saul was accompanied to Damascus by a party of men,[3] perhaps members of the Temple guard who were at the disposal of the High Priest,[4] and had been sent down to assist in securing the prisoners and bringing them to Jerusalem. The company knew themselves to be near the end of their journey, and after the hot noontide [5] ride under the open

[1] τὸ ἀκροατήριον (xxv. 23).

[2] See Bp. Chase's Hulsean Lectures on *The Credibility of the Acts*, p. 111 f. The evidence is opposed to the suggestion that S. Luke followed the practice of Thucydides in making his characters 'say what it seemed to him most opportune for them to say in view of each situation'; see Jebb, *Essays and Addresses*, p. 372.

[3] ix. 7 οἱ ἄνδρες οἱ συνοδεύοντες αὐτῷ, xxii. 9 οἱ σὺν ἐμοὶ ὄντες, xxvi. 13 τοὺς σὺν ἐμοὶ πορευομένους.

[4] Cf. Mc. xiv. 43, Jo. xviii. 3.   [5] περὶ μεσημβρίαν (Acts xxii. 6).

sky, welcomed the approach of the rich belt of vegetation that the ' rivers of Damascus' must always have thrown round the great city. Suddenly they were bathed in a light fiercer than that of an Eastern noon.[1]   All Saul's fellow-travellers saw it flash from the sky[2] and were struck down by the sight ;[3] and when they had again risen to their feet, all heard the sound which followed it.[4]   But in its inwardness the vision was only for Saul ; he alone saw, as it seems, a form,[5] and heard words addressed to himself into which the sound, as he listened, shaped itself.   What he first heard is given in identical terms by all the narratives : *Saul, Saul,*[6] *why persecutest thou me ?* and the question and answer which follow are also verbally the same in all : *Who art thou, Lord ?   I am Jesus, whom thou persecutest.*   The third account, however, adds to the Lord's first words, *It is hard for thee to kick against the goad.*   Whether the familiar Greek pro-verb[7] was uttered by the Speaker Himself, or is to

---

[1] xxvi. 13, ὑπὲρ τὴν λαμπρότητα τοῦ ἡλίου.

[2] xxii. 9 τὸ μὲν φῶς ἐθεάσαντο.

[3] xxvi. 14 πάντων καταπεσόντων ἡμῶν εἰς τὴν γῆν.

[4] ix. 7 ἱστήκεισαν ἐνεοί, ἀκούοντες μὲν τῆς φωνῆς.

[5] This is not distinctly stated in any of the accounts, but it appears to be implied in ix. 7 μηδένα δὲ θεωροῦντες, and see 1 Cor. ix. 1, xv. 8.

[6] Σαούλ, Σαούλ, not Σαῦλε, though Σαῦλος is used in vii. 58 ; viii. 1, 3 ; ix. 1, 8, and indeed throughout the narrative.

[7] See *e.g.* Aeschylus, *Agamemnon*, 1624.

be viewed as an interpretation which His words
afterwards received in the mind of Saul, matters
little ; they shew clearly enough the mental attitude
which he maintained to the moment when the vision
came.   Saul may have felt the prick of the goad
already when he listened to Stephen's last prayer ;
his conscience may have been uneasy then, and
perhaps it was uneasy now.   But he was too sure
of his ground to attend to any voice within ; it
needed a voice from heaven to give him peace.
What he now heard was from without and from
above ; it spoke with an authority he could not
resist.

The heavenly voice at once began to take effect.
The prostrate persecutor meekly asked, *What shall I
do, Lord ?* and the first step was pointed out, *Arise,
go into Damascus, and there it shall be told thee of
all things which are appointed for thee to do.*   With
absolute submission that step was taken ; blinded
by the light, the 'prisoner of the Lord'—for such he
already was—was led by the hand into Damascus,
and a lodging was found for him in the Straight
Street which still crosses the city from east to west.[1]
There three days afterwards he was found by one
of the brethren whom he had come to apprehend,
restored to sight, and baptized into Christ ; and in
Damascus he entered on the new life of witness

[1] See Hastings, *Dict. of the Bible*, i. 547[b] f.

to Christ which ended thirty years afterwards at Rome.

Not for an hour during those years of unremitting toil in the cause of the faith which once he 'devastated'[1] did S. Paul doubt the truth of the vision which turned his course right round, or hesitate to accept the consequences of his belief in it. Jesus of Nazareth was risen and at the right hand of God, as Stephen had said ; for had he not himself seen the Lord and heard His voice ? Jesus, then, was the Messiah, the Son of God, the Lord, and life was not too great a sacrifice to lay at His feet. There is no greater life in history than that which S. Paul spent in the service of Christ, and every act in it was what it was because S. Paul believed from the bottom of his heart that Jesus had appeared to him from heaven and sent him to do His work.

What was the nature of this appearance ? The conditions differ widely from those under which Stephen saw the ascended Christ. Saul, who lately breathed an atmosphere of menace and bloodshed,[2] was not filled, as Stephen had been, with the Spirit. There was in his case no ecstasy, no predisposition to see the invisible or to hear intelligible words when others perceived only a confused sound. He had no receptivity at this time for apocalyptic

---

[1] Gal. i. 23, ἐπόρθει.

[2] ix. 1 ἐνπνέων ἀπειλῆς καὶ φόνου.

visions of any kind, and an apocalypse of the risen
Christ was psychologically impossible for one who
up to that moment had honestly disbelieved in the
Messiahship of Jesus. A fierce flash of lightning out
of the blue might certainly have struck Saul blind,
while it only prostrated and dazed for the moment
those who were with him ; but what was there
to connect the flash in Saul's mind with the sight
of Jesus, to create the lifelong conviction that he
had seen the Lord? A prolonged clap of thunder
might have shaped itself in his imagination into
words, but why into those particular and most characteristic words, which left so clear an impression
that the three accounts, all more or less traceable
to S. Paul himself, have preserved them without
the slightest variation? Can it be seriously argued
that such thoughts as these : ' Jesus is the Lord
from heaven, and I am persecuting Him, and not
only these few followers of His at Damascus,' were
already seething in the persecutor's mind, needing
only a flash of lightning and a clap of thunder
to give them the force of a voice from the sky?
To suppose this is to go in the face of all our
accounts, which point clearly to a consistent rejection of Jesus by Saul up to the moment of the
appearance. It is equally out of the question to
represent the vision as a *replica*, a reminiscence,
under strong excitement, of the vision of Stephen.

That was a mental picture of the glory of the Lord in His heavenly state; in Saul's vision the glory shines round him on earth, and a voice sounds in his ears. Not a single feature in the two visions is the same.

But if what Saul saw and heard was not an apocalypse, nor the outcome of a state of ecstasy, nor a recollection of what Stephen claimed to have seen under such conditions, neither was it analogous to the appearances granted to the Eleven and others during the forty days. The Lord did not stand before Saul on the Damascus road and offer Himself to the touch of the persecutor or shew His hands and His side. If a form were seen in the blinding light, it was an appearance in the sky, not on the earth. If words were spoken, they were intelligible only to the person addressed. The whole transaction was in the sphere of the spirit, with the exception of the flash of light and the sound, of which all were cognisant. These might have been due to physical causes; but no physical cause, no merely psychological reason can explain the lifelong impression made on the robust mind of Saul.

One explanation and one only accounts for all the facts. It is to be found in the belief that Jesus Christ lives and works behind the veil of the visible order; that at the moment when Saul was about to enter upon a fresh course of disastrous hostility

to the faith, He exercised the authority which has
been committed to Him in heaven and on earth.
The vision which arrested Saul was not wholly sub-
jective; it was due to the direct action upon his
mind of a Force external to himself which he could
not resist, and in which he recognized the Person
of the risen Lord. Years after His final disappearance from the world, Jesus, he knew, had intervened
to bring His greatest enemy to a second birth: *last
of all, he appeared to me also, as if I had been the
abortion* of the Apostolic family.[1] To the consciousness of S. Paul himself that untimely birth was the
crowning evidence of the Resurrection. Other minds
may find it less convincing than the empty tomb,
or the appearances of the forty days; but when
all deductions have been made from the strength
of the Apostle's testimony, there remains in the
story a mystery to which his account of the
matter supplies the only key.

It has been said indeed that S. Paul's later history
shews him to have been peculiarly susceptible of
impressions created by visions and visitations of
the unseen. Twice after his conversion, during
the period covered by the Acts, he believed himself
to have seen the Lord or heard Him speak;[2] in
2 Cor. xii. he tells us that at one period of his life

[1] $\dot{\omega}\sigma\pi\epsilon\rho\epsilon\grave{\iota}\ \tau\hat{\omega}\ \dot{\epsilon}\kappa\tau\rho\acute{\omega}\mu\alpha\tau\iota$ (1 Cor. xv. 8).

[2] Acts xviii. 9 f., xxii. 17 ff.

I

the apocalypses he received were so numerous and splendid that he was in danger of being *exalted overmuch* by such experiences. But such revelations imply a receptivity in the mind of the person who is visited by them, of which Saul was at the time of his conversion wholly destitute. No one could have been more unprepared than he then was to receive an apocalypse of the risen and exalted Christ. There is nothing analogous between the circumstances of a zealous convert,[1] who is *caught up into Paradise,* where he hears *unspeakable words which it is not lawful for a man to utter,* and those of a bitter enemy of Christ who in the full tide of his career is arrested at noonday by a vision of which his fellow-travellers are partly cognizant. Moreover, it is clear that S. Paul himself places his later visions in a different category from the vision that caused his conversion. Such apocalypses were by no means peculiar to himself: they belonged to the spiritual exaltation of the Apostolic age,[2] and similar experiences have occurred in the lives of devout believers in all ages of the Church. But the appearance on the Damascus road was unique; it came to an unbeliever and

---

[1] The period referred to in 2 Cor. xii. was fourteen years before that Epistle was written, *i.e.* about 42, in the early days of Saul's preaching in Cilicia and at Antioch.

[2] Cf. 1 Cor. xiv. 6, 26, 30, and see the writer's *Apocalypse of S. John.*

turned him to faith.   He classed it with the appearances of the forty days,[1] for though it was not
purely an effect produced upon the mind, the light
and sound which accompanied the inward visitation
gave it a certain objectivity and a relation to the
phenomenal world.   It was the only vision which
he regarded in the light of evidence that could be
produced if the Resurrection were denied ; he never
appeals in this way to visions received during an
' ecstasy.'[2]   The Damascus vision was not the result
of an ecstatic condition of Saul's mind ; it was, if
we may believe his own account, supported by the
testimony of his life, a fact external to himself by
which he was convinced against his will and once
for all.   Once in early life it had been his lot *to
see the Righteous One and to hear a voice from his
mouth*,[3] and that sight and voice sufficed for all the
years that followed.

---

[1] I Cor. xv. 8 ἔσχατον δὲ πάντων . . . ὤφθη κἀμοί.

[2] Acts xxii. 17 ἐν ἐκστάσει.   [3] Acts xxii. 14.

III.

TO JOHN.

AUTHORITY: Apoc. i. 10-17; v. 6-14; xiv. 1-5, 14-16; xix. 11-16.

SIXTY years had passed[1] since the day when Saul saw the Lord on the road to Damascus. The work of the great convert had long been done, and his last witness borne at the heart of the Empire. In Asia his mantle had fallen upon John, one of the survivors of the first generation, whether the Apostle of that name or a prophet known to the next age as 'the Elder.'[2] The times were full of menace for the Church, for Domitian was on the throne, and was pressing his claim to a worship which no Christian could render to a mortal man: the informer was abroad, and a general persecution seemed to be imminent throughout Asia.[3] Meanwhile John, as the leader of the Church in that province, had been seized and deported to the isle of Patmos, where he 'saw the Apocalypse.'[4]

---

[1] On the date see the writer's *Apocalypse of S. John*[2], p. xcix ff.
[2] *Ibid.* p. clxxiv ff.   [3] *Ibid.* p. lxxxv ff.
[4] Victorinus: 'quando haec Ioannes vidit erat in insula Patmos in metallum damnatus a Domitiano Caesare. ibi ergo vidit Apocalypsin.'

It was the 'Lord's Day,' the day of the week
on which the Lord had risen and first appeared
to the Eleven, the day on which week by week
the Churches were accustomed to meet and break
the bread which is the Body of the Lord, and
was given by Him at His own last supper.[1] John
in Patmos had no brethren with whom he could
partake of that 'One Bread.' The width of the
Icarian Sea separated him from Ephesus and Smyrna,
where the Churches of the saints were now assembled
in their places of meeting; he, the prophet, the
pastor of the Churches, was on a sea-girt isle, cut
off from communion and fellowship. As he stood
gazing across the water, present in spirit with the
brethren, or with heart uplifted to the Lord,[2] he
heard behind him a voice like a trumpet blast,
bidding him write what he saw and send it to
the Churches of Asia. Turning to see whence the
voice came, he saw a vision of the glory of the
exalted Christ. Seven golden lampstands[3] recalled
the seven-branched candelabrum which stood in the
Tabernacle, and again in the Temple at Jerusalem
in the days before the fall of the city, and represented the Churches which shone as lights in the
face of the heathen world. In the midst of the
lampstands, fulfilling His promise to be with the

---

[1] ἐν τῇ κυριακῇ ἡμέρᾳ: cf. I Cor. xi. 20 κυριακὸν δεῖπνον.

[2] ἐγενόμην ἐν πνεύματι.   [3] λυχνίαι: cf. Heb. ix. 2 ἡ λυχνία.

Church to the end of time, stood the risen Lord, still 'like a son of man,'[1] a glorified human form such as Stephen perhaps had seen at the right hand of God. But beyond the upright figure, the head, and hair, and eyes, and feet, and hands, there was little to identify the August Person whom S. John beheld with the Son of Man who had been seen in the days of His flesh, or even in the days which followed the Resurrection. All else was idealized, superhuman, scarcely imaginable. The robe reaching to the feet, high-girt with a golden girdle, is but the ceremonial dress of the priesthood or of royalty; but the head and hair, white as wool or snow; the eyes, flashing like flames of fire; the feet, like brass glowing as though it had come out of a furnace: the voice, like a trumpet-blast or the roar of a cataract; the hand, bearing in the open palm a bracelet of stars; the great double-edged sword issuing tongue-shaped from the mouth; the face, dazzling to look upon, like the orb of the mid-day sun—all these are features widely remote from any conception we can form of humanity. The idealism of the portrait is evident; any attempt at a realistic reproduction of the Apocalyptic Christ would be as offensive to the best principles of Christian art as it would be

---

[1] ὅμοιον υἱὸν ἀνθρώπου, not τὸν υἱὸν τοῦ ἀνθρώπου, or even ὅμοιον τῷ υἱῷ τ. ἀ.

false to the right conception of His ascended human nature. Nevertheless S. John's idealism serves a very useful end. It reminds us that the exalted humanity of the Lord is not to be measured by any human standard with which we are acquainted; that it is invested with inconceivable power, in virtue of which it is able to fulfil its work of ruling and guiding, as a universal Presence, the destinies of the Church throughout the world.

The vision of the glorified Christ in the first chapter of the Apocalypse is introductory to the messages to the Seven Churches which follow in the second and third chapters. In these messages the Supreme Pastor is seen overlooking all the Christian societies, protecting, correcting, strengthening, rewarding as each has need. As the Apocalypse proceeds He appears in other aspects. In the next vision the doors of the invisible world are opened,[1] and the Seer sees the Throne of the Divine Majesty, surrounded by all the company of heaven : the four and twenty Elders who represent the Universal Church, the four living creatures which stand for universal animated Nature, and the vast encircling hosts of the Angels of God. As in the first vision, the central figure is that of the ascended Lord, but He wears a widely different form. *In the midst of the Throne and of the four*

[1] *c.* iv. 1 ff.

living beings, and in the midst of the Elders, I saw a Lamb standing, as slain, having seven horns and seven eyes, which are the seven Spirits of God, eyes sent forth into all the earth. In the sequel the Lamb receives the adoration of the whole host of heaven, and, alone of all beings that possess a created nature, He is counted worthy to open the Book of the Divine purposes, and to unfold the long process of the world's history. Later in the book a Lamb, evidently the same, is seen standing on Mount Zion,[1] surrounded by a hundred and forty-four thousand who have been ransomed by Him from the earth, and who follow Him wherever He goes, and learn to sing the new song in praise of Redemption. The two pictures are complementary to each other. The first teaches that the exaltation of Jesus Christ has not broken His connexion with the past; He is the same Person who was crucified, and His Sacrifice continues in its great consequences, and is the basis of His present glory. From the second we learn that His heavenly life does not debar Him from active sympathy with His brethren in earth or in paradise. 'Mount Zion' is the sphere of the Church's life, wherever it may be passed, whether on earth or among the departed; *ye are come unto Mount Zion, unto the City of the Living God,*[2] is true of all the members

[1] *c.* xiv. 1 ff.   [2] Heb. xii. 22.

of the Church who are here with us, as well as of the *spirits of just men made perfect*. The hundred and forty-four thousand have the Lamb in their midst wherever they are called to follow Him.

Another vision succeeds which restores to the Lamb His likeness to the sons of men.[1]   He is now seen throned on a white cloud, the symbol of His visible return ;[2] He is coming to reap the harvest of the earth, and in His hand he holds a sharp sickle, as the emblem of His work.   It belongs to Him not only to break one by one the seals of the closed roll of the future, but when all have been broken, when the history of the race stands open and complete, to gather up the results, good and evil, of the long process by which mankind has been ripened for its next stage of existence.   The risen and ascended Lord is the Judge of Men, and the delays of judgement are due only to the need of a longer interval to mature the produce of the world.

But before the harvest is reaped the Lord appears in another character.   Once again heaven is opened, and the Seer sees Him descend as the Victorious Word of God.[3]   The eyes of flame and the sharp sword of His mouth mark Him as the same person

---

[1] Apoc. xiv. 14 ὅμοιον υἱὸν ἀνθρώπου.   The singular formula of i. 13 is repeated.

[2] Cf. Acts i. 11, Apoc. i. 7.   [3] Apoc. xix. 14 ff.

who at the beginning of the Apocalypse appeared in the character of Priest and King of all the Churches. Now, however, his business is not with the Church, but with her adversaries. He rides the white horse of the conqueror : He is followed by the armies of heaven, mounted in like manner. He has come to rule the nations with the iron rod of an inevitable sway, and to destroy the rival powers of falsehood and blasphemy.[1] He bears the great name *King of kings and Lord of lords* ; on His head are many diadems,[2] tokens of an imperial power wider and more manifold than the power of the Caesars.

One aspect of the ascended life remains, but the Seer of the Apocalypse was not permitted to see it, or if he was, he has left it undescribed. The book ends with a magnificent picture of the New Jerusalem, which is seen *coming down out of heaven from God, made ready as a bride prepared for her husband.*[3] Her husband is the exalted Christ : in the days of His flesh He *gave himself for her*, and now He is coming to receive her unto Himself : *The marriage of the Lamb is come, and his wife hath made herself ready.*[4] But though the Bride appears, and is depicted at length, there is no vision of the Bridegroom. The revelation of the Divine Bridegroom belongs to the future, and the

[1] Apoc. xix. 20.   [2] διαδήματα πολλά.   [3] xxi. 2.   [4] xix. 7.

Seer pauses on the brink of that unimaginable appearing. *The appearing of the glory of the great God and our Saviour Jesus Christ*[1] is beyond the power even of the prophet of the Apocalypse to conceive ; Apocalyptic methods of representing the future or the invisible fail in view of that last disclosure. In the visions of the Priest-King, the Lamb, the Reaper, the Conqueror, S. John has shed all the light that can as yet be shed upon the mystery of the exalted Life. There is more, infinitely more, to be seen and known in regard to it, but not now : *Now we see through a mirror, darkly, but then face to face.*[2] The enigmas of our Lord's risen and ascended state will find their solutions when we ourselves have learnt to *bear the image of the Heavenly.*[3] What we know not here we shall know hereafter.

[1] Tit. ii. 13.   [2] I Cor. xiii. 12 δι' ἐσόπτρου ἐν αἰνίγματι.

[3] I Cor. xv. 49 φορέσωμεν καὶ τὴν εἰκόνα τοῦ ἐπουρανίου. The reading φορέσωμεν (WH) suggests that the earlier stages of the change may be reached while we are here.

MAKE THEM TO BE NUMBERED WITH THY SAINTS
IN GLORY EVERLASTING.

POSTSCRIPT.

In a considerable number of passages the New Testament speaks of an appearance of Jesus Christ which belongs to the future life, or to the end of the present 'age' and the ages that are to follow it. It may not be uninteresting to examine these passages and consider what they have to tell us of the hopes entertained by the Church of the Apostolic age.

There is (1) a strongly attested belief that at His Return the Christ will be seen by the whole world, by His enemies as well as by His friends. For this there was support in more than one explicit saying attributed to the Lord Himself. To Caiaphas and to the Sanhedrin he said, *Ye shall see the Son of Man sitting at the right hand of power, and coming with the clouds of heaven.*[1] On an earlier occasion, in an apocalyptic passage, we have the words, *Then shall they see the Son of Man coming in clouds with great power and*

[1] Mc. xiv. 62. So Mt., prefixing ἀπ' ἄρτι. Lc., who for ἀπ' ἄρτι has ἀπὸ τοῦ νῦν, drops ὄψεσθε.

glory.[1]   This is echoed by the writer of the Apocalypse, with the graphic addition, *And every eye
shall see him, and they which pierced him*.

This final manifestation to the world, with or
without the special reference to unbelievers, is
repeatedly mentioned in the Apostolic writings.
It is announced in the Angels' message on the
hill of the Ascension : *this Jesus . . . shall so
come in like manner as ye beheld him going
into heaven*.[2]   St. Paul's Epistles are full of it,
especially the earliest and the latest : *the Lord
himself shall descend from heaven, with a shout,
with the voice of the archangel, and with the trump
of God ;*[3] *at the revelation of the Lord Jesus from
heaven with the angels of his power in flaming
fire ;*[4] *until the appearing of our Lord Jesus Christ,
which in its own times he shall shew, who is the
blessed and only Potentate ; I charge thee . . . by
his appearing and his kingdom ; looking for the
blessed hope and appearing of the glory of our great
God and Saviour Jesus Christ*.[5]   S. Peter holds by
the same hope : *at the revelation of Jesus Christ*.[6]

But (2) the Church of the Apostles knew also

[1] Mc. xiii. 26, and see Lc. ; Jo. adds a reference to Zech. xii. 12
(cf. Apoc. i. 7).

[2] Acts i. 11.   [3] 1 Th. iv. 16.

[4] 2 Th. i. 7 f., 1 Tim. vi. 14 f., 2 Tim. iv. 1.

[5] Tit. ii. 13.   [6] 1 Pet. i. 7.

of a future revelation of Christ which was only for the faithful, and which was to be theirs, as it seems, in perpetuity.   Sometimes the dead in Christ are viewed as already in His immediate Presence : *knowing that whilst we are at home in the body, we are absent from the Lord (for we walk by faith, not by sight), we are . . . willing rather to be absent from the body, and to be at home with the Lord ;* [1] *to me to live is Christ, and to die is gain . . .   I am in a strait betwixt the two, having the desire to depart and be with Christ, for it is very far better.*[2]   But the actual vision of the Lord is connected, as it appears, with the great future which the Parousia will open.   There is some (perhaps intentional) ambiguity in such words as those of Christ on the night before He suffered : *Again a little while and ye shall see me ; I will see you again, and your heart shall rejoice,*[3] for they may be taken to refer to the return from the tomb or to the dispensation of the Spirit.[4]   But the more distant future seems certainly to be in view in the prayer, *Father, that which thou hast given me, I will that where I am, they also may be with me ; that they may behold my glory which*

[1] 2 Cor. v. 6 f.   [2] Phil. i. 21, 23.   [3] Jo. xvi. 16, 22.
[4] Cf. Westcott on S. John *ad loc.*: "the beginning of the new vision was at the Resurrection ; the potential fulfilment of it was at Pentecost . . . the spiritual Presence . . . will be caused by the Return."

thou hast given me.[1]   And it is clearly of the future that S. John writes : *We know that if he shall be manifested, we shall be like him, for we shall see him even as he is* ;[2] and again in the Apocalypse, *His servants shall do him service, and they shall see his face, and his name shall be on their foreheads.*[3]   *Then [we shall see],* S. Paul adds, *face to face.*[4]

How are these great hopes of the earliest Church to be interpreted in the light of modern knowledge and thought ?

In the first place it must be noted that all the passages which are quoted above refer to modes of life of which we have as yet no experience. We know nothing, except by conjecture or inference, of the capacities for vision or apprehension possessed either by departed spirits or by spirits clothed in a spiritual body. In reference to these stages of existence the New Testament expresses itself in the terms of our present life, or if it departs from these, the alternative is to use a symbolism which carries us but little further. The question to be determined is what were the substantial beliefs and expectations which the earliest believers entertained with regard to a future manifestation of Christ.

[1] Jo. xvii. 24.
[2] 1 Jo. iii. 2.
[3] Apoc. xxii. 3 f.
[4] 1 Cor. xiii. 12.

Two modes of 'seeing the Lord' were within the reach of the primitive Church after the coming of the Spirit. There was (1) the spiritual sight of faith, which had taken the place of ocular evidence. It is to this, perhaps, that the Lord chiefly refers when He speaks of seeing the Eleven again after His departure and being seen by them. The 'eyes of their hearts' were, as S. Paul says, 'enlightened'[1] by the Spirit, and they rejoiced (so S. Peter adds) *with joy unspeakable.*[2] *Looking unto Jesus the author and perfecter of* their *faith* they ran *with patience the race that* was *set before them.*[3] Their realization of the hidden life of Jesus Christ with God was so thorough and constant that it not only inspired a joy which no man could take from them,[4] but controlled their lives, causing them to endure to the end. But (2) besides the vision of faith, there was given to some—at first, perhaps, to not a few—the singular power of isolating themselves from phenomena, and anticipating the unseen and eternal in such wise that they knew not at the time whether they were 'in' the body or 'outside'[5] it. In this state of 'ecstasy,' as it was called,[6] *visions*

---

[1] Eph. i. 18 πεφωτισμένους τοὺς ὀφθαλμοὺς τῆς καρδίας ὑμῶν.

[2] 1 Pet. i. 8.   [3] Heb. xii. 2.   [4] Jo. xvi. 22.

[5] 2 Cor. xii. 2 εἴτε ἐν σώματι οὐκ οἶδα, εἴτε ἐκτὸς τοῦ σώματος.

[6] ἔκστασις (Acts x. 10, xi. 5, xxii. 17).

K

and revelations of the Lord[1] were sometimes granted ;
such, at least, was S. Paul's experience at a
particular time in his life,[2] and he was probably
not singular in this respect. Two other instances
have been given already,[3] and it is unnecessary to
pursue the matter further here.

Perhaps the 'ecstasy' of the first age may carry
us some way towards an understanding of what is
meant by the faithful departed being 'with the
Lord.' The Apostle, when in an ecstatic condition,
knew not whether he was still in the body ; he was
conscious of a detachment from external things such
as we connect with the state of the disembodied.
Moreover, he was *caught up into Paradise*,[4] the
counterpart of that garden of the Lord where
primaeval man could hear the voice of God walking among the trees, when the long hot day
was over, and the cool breeze of evening[5] brought
refreshment and increase of vital power. It is
remarkable that the same word is used by our
Lord in reference to His own meeting after death
with the spirit of the penitent robber : *To-day,
shalt thou be with me in Paradise* ;[6] and, again,

---

[1] 2 Cor. xii. 1 ὀπτασίας καὶ ἀποκαλύψεις Κυρίου.

[2] See p. 129 f.   [3] See pp. 117, 133 ff.   [4] 2 Cor. xii. 4.

[5] Gen. iii. 8. Heb. 'in the wind of the day,' LXX τὸ δειλινόν.
Dr. Driver (*Genesis*, p. 46) compares Cant. ii. 17 (R.V.), and con-
trasts Gen. xviii. 1.

[6] Lc. xxiii. 43 ἐν τῷ παραδείσῳ.

when in the Apocalyptic message He promises the conqueror that he shall eat of the Tree of Life which is in the midst of the spiritual Eden.[1]   All this may seem to point to some analogy between the ecstatic state and the state of 'them that depart hence in the Lord'; the latter are in fact, as the former in effect, 'outside the body,' and the spirit, now wholly 'delivered from the burden of the flesh,' realizes, as here we cannot realize, the Presence of God and the glory of Christ in the fellowship of the Holy Spirit, and is refreshed and quickened by what it sees.   The vision is purely spiritual, but it is real, and it is beatific.   *Blessed are the dead which die in the Lord.*

The prolonged ecstacy of the disembodied spirit will, in the belief of the Apostolic age, be broken at length by the coming of the Lord and the resurrection of the dead.   What is meant by 'resurrection' in this sense?   Not resuscitation, as many of the teachers of the ancient Church supposed;[2] but as S. Paul teaches, the clothing of the spirit with a spiritual body.   The 'bare grain' and the green blade of corn are so dissimilar that no one who had seen the former only could conceive of the latter. Equally inconceivable is 'the body that shall be.' But among its faculties it will assuredly have one which will answer to our sense of sight, the power of

[1] Rev. ii. 7.   [2] See the writer's *Apostles' Creed*, p. 93 ff.

conveying to the spirit impressions more perfect than any which the spirit by itself can form of the glory of the spiritual body of the Lord.

The revelation of Christ through the risen body will be, at the moment of His Coming, world-wide. So the Lord Himself seems to teach, and so the Apostolic age believed. To the unholy it may come in the flash of a terrible conviction that they have rejected Infinite Love and Beauty. To the faithful it will be a transfiguring power, which will complete their assimilation to the Master: *We shall be like him, for we shall see him*; the risen body will be *conformed to the body of his glory*; there will be in some way as yet unintelligible a *revealing of the sons of God*, coinciding with the final manifestation of the Only Begotten Son: *when Christ, who is our life, shall be manifested, then shall ye also with him be manifested in glory.*[1]

But the last revelation is not limited by the New Testament to the 'Day of the Lord,' whatever sense we may attach to that term. Beginning at a particular epoch, or, as it is sometimes represented, at a particular moment, brief as the twinkling of the eye,[2] it is not to be measured by days or years. There will be no subsequent withdrawal of the Presence of Christ, no vanishing of the light, no interval of

[1] I Jo. iii. 2; Phil. iii. 21; Rom. viii. 29; Col. iii. 4.
[2] I Cor. xv. 52 ἐν ἀτόμῳ, ἐν ῥιπῇ ὀφθαλμοῦ.

occultation, short or long. We shall *ever be with the Lord*,[1] living with perfect powers of vision and fellowship in the sight of the Divine Man, who is the Image of the invisible God.

This was the hope which inspired the age of the Apostles. To our own age it may seem chimerical, because we have no powers by which it can be analysed, and no experience to which it can be compared. Yet experience shews that when this hope has been sincerely embraced it raises and controls human life with a strength which no other motive can exert. Tens of thousands in all generations since the first century have lived *soberly and righteously and godly in this present world, looking for the blessed hope* of our eternal life in the Presence of Christ. *Every one that hath this hope set on him purifieth himself, even as he is pure.*[2]

[1] I Th. iv. 17.   [2] Tit. ii. 12 f., I Jo. iii. 3.

INDEX

Absolution, 38.
Adam, the Last, 33.
All hail, 11 n.
Apocalypse, the, 132 ; 'apocalypse,' 129 f., 145 f.
'Apostles,' 31 ; their mission,
100 f.
Ascension, the day of, 92 n.; place
of, 103 ; the event, 104 ff. ;
vision of Christ after, 113 ff. ;
'ascension,' 104.
'authority,' 70 f., 129.

baptism, Christian, 73 ff.
Barjonah, 59.
Bethany, 103.
'binding' and 'loosing,' 36.
*blessed are the dead which die in
the Lord*, 147.
*blessed are they that have not
seen*, 48 f.
bridegroom, Christ as, 138.

Christ, the risen : changes of
form, 22 ; disappearance, 23 f. ;
body not docetic, 28 f.
Church, rapid growth of, after
Pentecost, 113.
Cleopas, 17.
Conqueror, vision of the, 137 f.
'consummation,' 81 f.
conversion of Saul, accounts of
the, 122 f.
Corinth, the first letter of St.
Paul to, xii, 83.
creed, the old Roman, 105.

Damascus, 121, 124 f.
'disciple,' to, 73 n.
documents, xi ff., xv f.
doubt, honest, 48.

Easter Day, appearances on the
first, 40.
'ecstasy,' 117, 129 f., 133 ff.,
145 f.
Emmaus, 17, 26 f.
ever with the Lord, 148 f.

faith as contrasted with sight,
49 f.
fish, the miracle of the, 56 f.
five hundred, the, 69, 82 ff., 85.

Galilee, return to, 51 ff., 67 ;
return from, 92.

'Hebrews,' 113 f. ; Gospel ac-
cording to the, xv, 29, 89 f.
'Hellenists,' 113 f.
Hort, Dr., 43.

Ignatius, 29 n.

James, the Lord's brother, xii,
86 ff.
Jerusalem, the starting point of
Christian missions, 97, 100.
Joanna, 1.
Johannine ideas, 31.
John, 5 f., 57, 64 ; Gospel of S.,
xiii, xvi, 51, 55 ; appendix to,
54 n.
Joppa, the road to, 17 n., 21

Lamb, the, visions of, 135 ff.
Levi, 54.
'Lord's Day,' the, 133.
Luke, S., Gospel according to, xi, xiii, xvi f., 3, 27 n., 51, 53, 103 ff.

Mark, S., Gospel according to, xiii, xvi f., 3, 51, 92, 99 n. ; appendix to, xiii f., 22, 29, 78 f.
Mary of Magdala, 1, 5, 6 ff., 11 n., 13, 16, 39.
Matthew, S., Gospel according to, xiii, xvi, 3, 11, 67, 91 ; text of Mt. xxviii. 19, 74 n.
Messianic hope, the, 94 ff.
Mission of the Church, 30 ff., 71 ff.
'mountain,' 67.

'name, into the,' 74 ff.

Old Testament, interpretation of the, 20 f., 27, 93 ff., 115 f.
Oxyrhynchus sayings, the, xvi.

'paradise,' 130, 146.
'parousia,' the, 65, 143.
pastoral office, the, 61 f., 66.
Patmos, 132.
Paul, S., his evidence, xii, xvi, 82 ; visions after his conversion, 129 f.
peace be unto you, 28, 30.
Peter, S., 4 ff., 13 ff., 39, 46, 56 ff., 59 ff., 61 f. ; 'visited' by S.

Paul, xii, 14 ff. ; Gospel of, xv, 54 f.
Priest-King, vision of the, 133.
'Psalms,' the, 94.

Rabbuni, 7.
Reaper, vision of the, 137.
Renan, 16, 84.
'right hand of God,' 106, 117.

Salome, 1.
Sanhedrin, the, 27, 115, 120.
Saul, 120 ff., 126 ff.
sins, 'remitting' and 'retaining,' 36 ff.
Spirit, the Holy, 32 ff., 76 f., 79 f., 82, 98 f., 145.
spiritual body, the, 50, 147 f.
Stephen, 114 ff. ; his vision, 117 ff.

Temple guard, the, 123.
Tertullian, 63.
Testament of our Lord, xvi.
Thomas, S., 41 ff., 48, 55 ; Acts of, 42.
touch me not, 8 f., 39, 50.
Trinity, the doctrine of the Holy, 76 ff.

upper room, the, 102.

women, the, at the Cross and the Tomb, 1 ff. ; appearance to, 11 f.
Word of God, the, 137.

Made in United States
North Haven, CT
23 May 2022

19449101R00095